Life is a Fatal Disease

Life is a Fatal Disease
Collected Poems 1962–1995

by
Paula Gunn Allen

West End Press

Acknowledgments are due to the following:

Books:
The Blind Lion (Berkeley: Thorp Springs Press, 1975); *Coyote's Daylight Trip* (Albuquerque: La Confluencia, 1978); *A Cannon Between My Knees* (New York: Strawberry Press, 1981); *Star Child* (Marvin, South Dakota: Blue Cloud Press, 1981); *Shadow Country* (Los Angeles: UCLA–American Indian Center Press, 1982); *Wyrds* (Santa Fe: Taurean Horn, 1987); *Skins and Bones* (Albuquerque: West End Press, 1988).

Periodicals:
The American Voice, *Yefief*, *Studies in American Indian Literature*.

First edition, February 1997
ISBN 0-931122-85-6

Front cover by Paula Gunn Allen
Back cover photograph of the author by Tama Rothschild Photography
Typography by Prototype, Albuquerque, NM

This project is supported in part by a grant from the National Endowment for the Arts, a federal agency.

Distributed by the University of New Mexico Press.

West End Press • P.O. Box 27334 • Albuquerque, New Mexico 87125

A Measure of Difference

They all
saw an elephant
all
got the idea
of elephantness

but they all saw it
differently—
such is the beauty
of elephants.

Corrales, 1965

CONTENTS

Part I: THE WARNING

Part II: BIRTH IS 100% FATAL

Part I

THE WARNING

SURGEON GENERAL'S WARNING: Smoking by Pregnant Women May
Result in Fetal Injury, Premature Birth, and Low Birth Weight.

Malinalli, La Malinche, to Cortés, Conquistador

And among other gifts of tribute the now-subdued people of the
Maya coast gave to Cortés their choicest girls, and among these the slave-
girl, Malinal. . . .
It was in March 1519 that the people of Tabasco gave the Lady
Marina (as Bernal Diaz always speaks of her) to the strangers, and this was
in the shadowland country at the far frontier of the Aztec confederacy. . . .
Throughout the first march on Mexico, after they were joined by
Malinal, the Spanish were forced to fight in only one instance. . . .
Otherwise the road of their first penetration into the country . . . was
paved by a string of diplomatic victories as remarkable as so many straight
passes at dice.

— William Brandon

Ever I twisted you to my will,
oh the great bringer of the goddess' wrath,
for you did not know that she sang
of your victories before your name was dreamed,
before your flesh was formed.
Ah, you marched, brazen and satisfied,
certain of your cunning and your strength,
and of your place before all of the gods,
straight for the heart of my chief enemy,
he who gave his life and gold in fear,
but in certain knowledge of his part:
only you, unblessed conqueror,
father of my son, remained ignorant,
boastful of a power you would never own.
You stride the continents of your fool's pride
not knowing why it is I, Malinche, whose figure
looms large above the tales of your conquests.

The Spaniard has a disease for which
the only cure is gold, you said; nor
did you know the disease was more of the spirit
than of the flesh: you thought to mock
the piety of him who bowed before you,
of him who was my enemy, my companion,
my beloved Moctezuma. He gave you
all the gold you sought, unprotesting.
Did you ever think to wonder why?
Or how could it be that you,
paltry in your barbaric splendor,

alone could ride
across the jungles and the hills
to the heart of Áztlan?
Did you never wonder who it was
that led you, let you in?
Did you never wonder why?

And I myself have been maligned: a fitting
irony. Maligned I, La Malinche,
chief of traitors, chief of slaves.
Betrayed I the father gods,
the false serpent who claimed
wings, who flew against
the grandmother sun declaring
prior right; who brought
murder and destruction, gold and jade;
who dreamed of war as tribute
for his blood-drenched kings.
And knowing this, still
I prayed to the mother of us all,
she of sun and star who gives
both life and light,
anguished did I pray to the serpent
woman who lies coiled and still, waiting.

The hour is late, Cortés.
And just as I stood
and watched you strip great
Moctezuma of his gold, just as I stood
guiding your words and your soldiers
with my gaze as I had guided them
with my many-flavored tongue,
I now stand, silent, still,
and watch with great Cihuacoatl
as your time runs out.
Listen: in the barrios even now I hear
her wailing cry as it was heard
in the chambers of the ruler a cycle ago:
oh, my beloved children,
where will I hide you?
Look into the holy mirror that you stole
from him, who you murdered for his will:
see if in its depth you can find my face,
glimpse the falling feathers
of your dying king.

For Carol

the moon, solitary in the dusk
the dark, growing in power
what you are to become, alone.

our children
              (as we
                      the glazed afternoon sky
                                  evening rising soft and kind
                in the darkened evening elms
                      singing silently

                                impossibly
                                      secure

                            a vision
                                    maybe
                          unrecognized
                          balanced
                                in un-
                                          musical
                                                guitars)

will not remember evening as it appeared to us
purple and cool   annihilating mountains
as it came   fire and clear air
to our eyes

Pocahontas to Her English Husband, John Rolfe

In a way, then, Pocahontas was a kind of traitor to her people. . . .
Perhaps I am being a little too hard on her. The crucial point, it seems to
me, is to remember that Pocahontas was a hostage. Would she have
converted freely to Christianity if she had not been in captivity? There is
no easy answer to this question other than to note that once she was free
to do what she wanted, she avoided her own people like the plague. . . .
Pocahontas was a white dream—a dream of cultural superiority.
—Charles Larson
American Indian Fiction

Had I not cradled you in my arms,
oh beloved perfidious one,
you would have died.
And how many times did I pluck you
from certain death in the wilderness—
my world through which you stumbled
as though blind?
Had I not set you tasks,
your masters far across the sea
would have abandoned you—
did abandon you, as many times
they left you
to reap the harvest of their lies.
Still you survived, oh my fair husband,
and brought them gold
wrung from a harvest I taught you
to plant. Tobacco.
It is not without irony that by this crop
your descendants die, for other
powers than you know
take part in this as in all things.
And indeed I did rescue you—
not once but a thousand thousand times
and in my arms you slept, a foolish child,
and under my protecting gaze you played,
chattering nonsense about a God
you had not wit to name. I'm sure
you wondered at my silence, saying I was
a simple wanton, a savage maid,
dusky daughter of heathen sires

6

who cartwheeled naked through the muddy towns
learning the ways of grace only
by your firm guidance, through
your husbandly rule:
no doubt, no doubt.
I spoke little, you said.
And you listened less,
but played with your gaudy dreams
and sent ponderous missives to the throne
striving thereby to curry favor
with your king.
I saw you well. I
understood your ploys and still
protected you, going so far as to die
in your keeping—a wasting,
putrefying Christian death—and you,
deceiver, whiteman, father of my son,
survived, reaping wealth greater
than any you had ever dreamed
from what I taught you and
from the wasting of my bones.

Medicine Song

The Hexagram

> I add my breath to your breath
> That our days may be long on the Earth;
> That the days of our people may be long;
> That we shall be one person;
> That we may finish our roads together.
> May Oshrats bless you with life;
> May our life roads be completed.

—Laguna Pueblo

In this room where voices spin the light
making webs to catch forbidden visions
(center that cannot be grasped) climb
ladders that do not reach the sky,
hands do not touch,
glances unmet rise, fall
gracelessly against shadows that hold
the song inside, tongueless celebration
of what is absurd. Light follows dark,
(helpless voices climb) as though
precious life could be so stilled,
as though a flicker of mind could turn
hurt or terror into this night's
entertainment. The woman next to me
clutches knees to chest
shrinks into a corner of the room
as though she could disappear,
gracefully evade the web
that grows around us.

The wall becomes a solid past:
no unexpecteds here her shoulders
seems to say, and hurt that is not hers
feels out the room, voices climb,
spiral, spin toward finity,
sing obstinately.

The Judgment

On the webbed finger of a water dream
swims one who is named Child of the Lake—
foolish emblem on the bare surface of the dream.
(Finger of time pointed at my face
as though some unheard shame had dowsed my mind)
and this is unexpected. I have known my shadow
lurked just out of reach, but that it should
confront my sight in crystal clarity,
turning into a shadowed burial place,
making of dream absurdity—agh, but I
saw the Katsina's duck-billed face turn toward me,
heard his words, misunderstood their sounding
and became,
as swift as waters bearing him from me,
plaything of a mind half gone.

The Image

Long (as song so stricken goes)
I've worn the crown of penitence
on my tongue, a layering of cloud
familiar to my eyes
(that is the sign of Katsina-kind)
and long have told the songs
and tales of Kawaik
how I might make of wandering a reason
an image of a sacred ladder I might climb
as earth and water climb to help
the wingless fish upstream.
But in a room of solid sound,
where shame is emblem
and fear its hopeless twin,
the voices that climb upsong
can only make blank utterance
that grows to blind dream.

The Lines

child of water
desert mind
broken strands floating
on the surface of the lake
still body so small
the damage barely shows
small thing
unable to spin
turn in your death
shadow too stricken to flow
dream in your silent shadow
celebrate.

Albuquerque, 1971

Something Fragile, Broken

1.

i had seen something
i had wanted

and sorrow is not to enter
into it:

a sparrow falling: a tiny
fragile egg, crushed

it was in the grass then
fallen, dead.

reached out, that hand,
palm open, such care

fallen anyway, all the way
to the ground

where it smashed.
the slate stones that ringed

the lily pond of my grandmother
held it, blue and broken.

sorrow was not to enter
into it. but it did.

and i am not stone but shell,
blue and fragile. dropped,

i splatter. spill the light
all over the stone

nothing that can be mended.

2.

sorrow was not to enter this

but it did. and i
was not to weep, or

think such things or
let you see that this,

which was not to be entered,
was born and broken before

entering. not in tears
exactly, not fallen in

that way, but still.
and i knew what would not

be spoken. a circle that
would not be broken

shattered anyway, or died.
like ripples on the lake,

when the stone has sunk
deep beneath the surface,

die. sorrow has no part
in it. some things just

don't go on. some circles
come undone. some sparrows

fall. sometimes sorrow,
in spite of resolution,

enters in.

What It Means

what it means, a beckoning
soft lighted house, door
suddenly thrown open
inviting

what it means, a stranger entering,
watched by others unseen,
who call your name, causing
trembling

what it means, a woman
veiled, eyes slow to adjust
to the light, slow to lift your veil
wondering

what it means, a word plummeting
lands hard on your shoulder,
talons tearing through muscle to bone
mutilating

what it means, the beckoning
turned to distance, warmth become
hard and cold,
forbidding

what it means, the others
turned to ungiving stone
the woman with her face exposed
shoulder oozing

what it means
unseen
caught open in a moment
that closed

San Pablo, May 24, 1986

The Garden

sky still bright
we weed, companionable.
she on her side of the low wall
me on mine
"they leave their shells in the ground"
she says, "see these holes? I don't know
why, they have to be dug up and
thrown away." she holds up
a transparent thing,
tissue pattern for an insect dress.
her petunias, my corn, beans, squash and I
nod amiably.

in the hills last night
two more animals
dismembered:
rectum, lip, nostril, vagina
split.
bodies left bloodless
on the unmarked grass.
something out there.
something unknown.
I straighten, groaning
wipe sweat from my eyes.
mystic impulse all around
slicing holes in air
digging bad dreams
in daylight.
sun like a corpse over me.
sky blooming deep.
a shroud.

scene ii

unmannered.
soft as night.
air keening.
sky building.
what manners these?

fear lightly easing itself over
back wall, through trees.
starshine
beginning at the edge.
her dress moves with ease, eyes
glitter, hair
so soft in evening wind, she
recalls summer nights,
arms like branches singing, body
sinking graceful into dusk.
comfort of lounge chair
holds buttocks, back, pliant neck.
she dreams of Pentecost, tongues
of flame above her shining hair,
longs for beatitude, so suited
to this place.
a manner of speaking touches her lips
lightly, careful for her carelessness,
words slip cautiously toward formation,
birds settle in for the night, crying.

daylight evaporates as she swirls
her drink, sips cold with perfect ease
against her teeth, rests against cushions
soft as dissolving clouds
overhead.
trees by the back wall
begin to stir
ominous.
sky goes dark.
she doesn't see,
she doesn't make a sound.
Pentecost shimmers
flows from her hair
between her thighs.

scene iii

light angling
volunteer's face ashen
up two days and nights
starshine is not what
got in her eyes.
he used a knife

on her vagina she tells me,
and maybe the hatchet we found
beside the bed
the blood, my god, she tells me.
outside surgery we stand
uneasy, graceless, longing
for the carelessness of birds.

scene iv

haunted
tissue paper hulls
bad dreams in daylight
no sleep in dark
before my eye
a shadow
photograph of Brazilian
Indian woman hung
by the ankles from a pole
long hair sweeping down
blowing in the laden breeze
white hunter standing next to her
spread legs. she is naked.
she is dead.

On the Street: Monument

On the day Fuad died the heat
glittered and melted the asphalt; someone
in Cambridge thought Marx understood the plight
of streets and watered poor hearts of brown, black and gold
masses: proletariat, confined to non-photographic modes
of thought.

I remember wondering how I could
not break; whether the butterfly in the shade of Fuad's
carefully concealed grave hole was a sign—and if
anything was ever sacralized. No matter what
ideologies occurred before that time, my
son was dead.
The good do not deserve anything more
than their virtue. The evil
inherit the earth, regardless of what Marx
has said.

On the street
the commonplace is ideologue: so little time
spent hanging out, romantic shadows hide ivied eyes from spit
on the sidewalk, ground-in shit, sickening heat:
a street is going
someplace. Camera stays.
Nothing in the frame has any reason to be.

Wool Season: 1973

In Cubero
days too hot, arroyo dry
dust marks the road that forever crumbles at the edge
it will rain next month. Now
time to get the wool in—paid up, settled,
like in the good times when wool sold by the tons
even out of Cubero.
Now it's petrochemicals all the way, and the arroyo gets deeper
the road narrows a little every year.
Old Diego died in the bottom of the arroyo
a couple of years ago. They say he was drunk,
missed his way in the dark. They found him in the morning.
The old huge boulders I climbed have shattered and moved
downstream in summer floods. The heavy hum of fat flies is the same.

What do the people do when they can't sell their wool?
How do they settle for the lard and mutton and flour?
The kids' clothes, the ladies' shawls, the shovels,
tires and gas?
The wool lies heavy in the barn now, season after season,
unsold, unwanted. No one even tans the hides.
They can't survive much more. Being punished for no crimes.
The skin of my thought is bloody wool, stuffed
with gorging ticks like the packed sacks of fleece.
Don't play in the barn where the wool is stacked,
they used to warn us kids.
You'll be killed whether you've murdered anyone or not.

A Chloroformed Poem to Your Closed Eyes

Why is my face all wrong
turned away (as they say) set?
A heart turned away from itself should not
waver on empty shores
                        (blinding)
pull on the unseeing cliff   (wish)
wash eternally benevolent scattered quartz
                                    (sand).

The long shores of last evening (or twenty years ago)
set my head in rubies and pearls   (the dream)
shaking me
                (maracas)
                    (rattlesnakes)
            from ignominious nights.
Enormous boots, belly, beard, drunk,
"My name's Sam. I love you." Yesterday
nothing happened in spite of diamond ravings
                                (blind)
                                (waves)
                                (weaving)
on a can-strewn moor, all the storms of perversity
(heaven) pulling our eyes earthward   (lies)
too many wash and wear tear-proof clothes. Nothing
could happen, we didn't undress, how
could we?
                (staggering)
Faces with the chance of meeting today
lost again. Say cheese awhile longer.   Freeze.
"Why   (whiskey)
don't you hear me   (rye)
say I love you?"

Can you confront rubies, encounter daisies, meet
with pearls?   (trembling)
                                are you a grimy
                                a grimmy
                                a shasta
                                who hasta
                                a granny
                                grin?

19

a drunken pledge is not a door.
I can't eat what isn't there
                              (drink)
but there
            or there
                . . . .
A promise unsaid, unthought, unheeded
                                    (needed)
is best.
(Last)
(Lost)

BULLSHIT

That's best.
                Don't learn from the words I give
                Don't lean on the words I learn

Rubies are rubbish.
So are pearls.
And I   (inlaid)
must hide my beard. And I
look strange in big boots. And I
(inland) can't grow a big belly
anymore   (beached)
Why not rubber pearls?

having opened ourselves
to closed doors and
locked bright windows
we are next.
                "I love you honey, but the bar's closed."

20

Curiosity at UD

(Photography in Literature in the Streets)

The other day in California
oops shot some poor innocent citizen
in his warm bed. Bet he was surprised.
Indians say Watergate is causing floods—
"Old Indian trick." Days go by.
(Want to read the headlines, Dick?)
The postman tells me it's all lies
and I should save my dime.
The guys hanging out on the corner are worldly
wise and timely jokes. Breakfast at noon
with shades of long-gone friends hanging out
around my chair as though I had daguerrotypes of them
in my pocket or
strung around my neck like the dowager queen.
Cataclysmic stirrings this morning. I
know my shadow is caught too many times, shreds
of me left in too many places, times, and there are
few pictures of me, almost all in the family—
imagine presidents—
taken everywhere, every day.

Albuquerque, 1973

21

Missing

all along
seeing friends
all distracted. come again,
they say, smiling at the air
beside my head.
then I am out again,
surrounded by the wet
wet green, going in circles,
finally lost,
missing the way
a hundred times
stopping in panic,
exhausted.

all the way east
across the continent
I've driven looking for gold,
finding green. and rain.
and missing the holes in the highway
the way.
aimless,
I travel in a futile try to reach
what is not there.
trees and sky
fall endless into rain.
people who smile into silence
disappear in my wake,
passing by.

in other places
there has been snow
endless and losing.
a confusion of emotion,
a stilling.
other times there was sky
and ordered mesas
mountains blue and self
contained around the edges,
bordering vision, holding me.
and color: brown

and lavender, gold
and red. blue gray white.
shaping. circling. holding within.

I am missing
solid places.
all these holes: two
thousand miles of them.
pits in the highway. bowls.
the roads pull away
from their centers,
running at the edge.

all the way back
before I entered the cloying
green, the preying, swollen sky,
I was bordered by children,
parents, mountains, home.
Now I think
about my daughter,
brown face falling
in tears. reaching,
missing, before I'd even gone.
and my father,
brown face softening
into tears,
reaching, finding
a hole where our hands
should meet
over two thousand miles.
call me every night, he says.
I am missing
my mother, quiet and dear
in the kitchen stirring things,
filling plates and cups,
glasses and bowls, not
reaching, keeping
busy, spinning me out
away from her
in thought beyond the door, only
after I've gone
reaching. I think of her
searching through magazines
my last night there

for a lost
recipe to send me on my way,
saying goodbye. I am
pulling away from them
running toward the edge,
trying to miss the holes.

Cazenovia, June 1982/
Los Angeles, January 1983

High Steppin' Seboyetano

the poplar tree at the end of the yard
in Cubero was tall and sweet. it wailed
stronghearted frail
in summer winds. it guarded
and it met. it stood
where the cement walk went narrow
just before it opened to the achingly
grassy yard

where on that lawn deep summer nights
years since or someplace else
grown-ups talking, chairs creaking,
cigarettes, cigars poling the dark
like secret phoenician barques. we
were children playing, my sisters
and i, listening with half a mind
to grown-ups talk, dreaming
of futures beneath other stars
drowsing safe on the damp lawn,
remembering in darkness the green
shivering in wonder when coyotes wailed
among the cedars on the sandstone hills
to find each other in the dark

and on some nights we went inside
and daddy danced so hard he'd make
our stone, adobe-plastered house shake
pine wood floor bound, pound
a tight stretched drum
to the charleston, he taught us
how to swing while mother played the piano
until at last she would rise
and we would put the records on
and together they would show us
how the real dance was done
how much life could wail
like tree caught in wind
when elegant india de Cubero
and suave arabe de Seboyeta
combined

and so some other times,
on other planets far away
unguarded by poplar tree,
we go inside compartments
whose cement doesn't open
on to anything, not
deep thick lawn, not coyotes wailing
on the closeby sandstone hills,
my sisters and i the grown-ups.
with half a mind our children listen
to our grown-ups' talk and
dream of futures among the stars,
drowse in weed and black jack air
wail on piano drum honky tonk
while mother holds herself
achingly aware
in makeup and party hair
listens with half a mind
and dreams of futures beyond the stars
drowses on the soft couch,
remembers in lamplight the dream

and daddy dances all alone
struttin', steppin' high, while sons,
grandsons, granddaughters wail
among old blues guitars
to find each other in the dark

and just outside the heavy door
undying cedars teach the city
winter wind to swing

Albuquerque, 1980

Heyoka, Coyote Tale

Alfonso's house is gone. There's
a space where it used to be. The
baile hall is fallen down, tin roof
rusted on the ground. The ghostly cattle
dance there now, from the looks of it.
Remember Alfonso? He was obscene. When I was seven
he asked if I would trade him
a doughnut for a banana. I didn't know
what he meant for some time. But
my girlfriend got mad when he said it,
and he leered, so I knew the drift.
He was obscene. I wonder if he's dead.
Maybe his ghost dances in the ruins
of the baile hall with the cows.
And I remember Pinky who had French
pictures the boys of Cubero sniggered over.
He was also obscene, but a lot younger,
and not to be confused with the Anglo Pinky,
the one who brought my uncle out. Neither
of them ever forgot it, and one day Pinky,
the Anglo one, tried to do a blow job
with a shotgun. It blew him away instead; left
his brains, pink I suppose and probably red,
splattered all over the walls
of the house his crazy old mother lived in alone
after she cleaned up the mess. Until she tried
her son's trick: it worked for her as well. That
house is still there, not fallen down
in the least, its windows covered
with galvanized tin, its dark green cement walls
fading but strong. It's on the road
out of Cubero, just on the edge
of the Laguna Reservation.
We ride past it on our way out of town.

El Cerrito, 1984

Never Cry Uncle

—for Ook

he liked the ones who would be friends—
the street kind, the hardtimers, the pals:
they were most often black, because he
was indian and there weren't so many
indian faggots around, and those there were—
well, I don't know, maybe he was over them.
maybe he'd gone through them, or,
most likely, they reminded him of home,
a fearful thought;
of his wife, an indian woman,
of his mother, likewise. but not so wise
was he. he kept gettin ripped off and bruised.
he kept drinkin too much. he
took too much valium, too much speed, too
much angel dust. too much acid.
too much mescaline.

he went sometimes to the indian center. went
sometimes to the powwows, all dressed up
pueblo indian style, bandanna rolled up and tied
around his head, thin pale hair drawn back,
ponytail style. earrings, necklace,
icecream pants, velvet shirt, blanket
over his arm. he looked swell.
but it depressed him to go there, even
the fry bread, even the good sweet corn. his
friends couldn't keep him from gettin hurt,
they tried. they spent as much time takin
care of him as they could.
and his family—us, his nieces, also exiled,
too far away from blood and home
to make sense. we kept his money when he asked;
we gave him some of it when he asked. we
got him out of jail when he asked. we took
him home. we all finally got tired of it,
though, locked as we were in our own blood
feuds, locked as we were in our own hardtimes
hustles, and streets, and trips, and friends.
he got beat bad, but he didn't die. he spoke
only Spanish instead. he refused

28

to remember how it had happened. forgot
it all and remembered only Lucky Strikes
and sometimes friends and beer. he got
locked up that way, and that way he got
loose. beat senseless he was,
and left for dead. but he didn't die.
just got locked up again. now he listens
to the hum forever buzzin in his head.
he only makes dumb indian jokes.
he only remembers his hardtimes friends.

San Pablo, 1984

Laguna Ladies Luncheon

—on my fortieth birthday

Gramma says it's so depressing—
all those Indian women,
their children never to be born
and they didn't know
they'd been sterilized.
See, the docs didn't want them
bothered, them being so poor and all,
at least that's what is said.
Sorrow fills the curve of our breasts,
the hollows behind the bone.
Three closet Indians
my mother, my grandmother and I
who nobody sterilized. Our
children are grown.
We do not dare to weep
over coffee in this elegant place;
quiet, we hold their grief unborn.
My mother says it's the same
as Nazi Germany.
A medical holocaust.
Now I'm officially
an old woman, she says,
I can tell them that.

Albuquerque, 1979

30

Grandma's Dying Poem

—for Aggie

When somebody dies
you have to consider.
When the last grandmother dies
you have to reflect.

She's somehow what your life has been
all along,
you realize—your life has been
a mirror of her ways, the reflection
slightly different by small changes
time and fashion make. When
her place is empty, do you move in?
Do you take her barking staccato
voice that modulates in a different key
to say what can be said (as so much can't)?
Do you forget, did she ever know to the bone
the delicacy of porcelain as her skin,
or seductive fall of lash,
beguiling coif to frame her face
the perilous fragility of lace
clasped fine with cameo
to grace a slender elegant length of neck
that was her own?
No, not for her a light fluting voice
or feminine coy
glance to pass down to me—
I could never step graceful
to frail dance any more than she
(though she might deny); the speed of Virginny Reel,
Corn Dance and Seboyeta Waltz were more our style—
But didn't she try? How she tried.

I wonder, grandma. I look
at your 18-year-old face
gazing steady out at me
from an 83-year-old photograph,
eyes softened by some photographer's ploy, fine
hair done smooth and plain
over turn-of-the-century rats
except for those fly-away wisps

you never could control
your soft hair, thicker then,
nearly gone by the time you died.
Hairiness not any part of your line, grandma,
not on any side:
no raven Indian princess locks to hang thick heavy
down your back, no graceful elegance of white
that ladies in your century's books wore like a crown
(or mine).

So what are we, if not the ladies
as you so long supposed? Or did you know?
Ladies don't look directly,
don't bark their words,
are not abrupt, determined,
demanding like you, like me. So
I am undone by the nature of genetic lines—
Or is it the force of learning, strong,
of knowing you all my life? After all
I grew up next door to you,
saw you every day my first seven years
before I went away to school,
and often enough afterward.
Surely I would have learned
from all that, grandma, how to be
a wanderer in an alien land,
a pretender to customs I cannot claim
just as I learned to listen for your breath
while I lay next to you not so long ago,
where we rested
safe in my mother's,
your daughter's house,
wondering if you slept
or simply waited,
like you waited all the long dark
days after you lost your sight,
your power to move and shape and hold,
your house, your garden, your music,
your soul, your life.
In those days you spent stalking your death
I wondered what you thought through
those obscure hours day and night,
what you waited for.
What fire burned in you?
(And it was a fire, I know.)

I think now about the ways I knew you:
presiding over a kitchen's clicking toaster,
butane stove those so many years ago,
burning trash in the rust red barrel,
burning breakfast napkins in the iron kitchen stove,
heaping coal into the dark
iron hole that kept us warm.
Or bending in your summer yard
over a tiny riot of flowers,
ever threatened by mutiny of weeds,
head held sturdy under broad straw hat
cotton shirt and slacks kept from grime
by a loose flowing smock
—or do I imagine that?
Didn't I see (how often)
you drag and whip miles of heavy hose to pour
precious desert water over mulched acres of dirt
until you could make them yield
to your tenacious pinto terrier will?
I would have learned from that, grandma, I suppose.
That would be something I wouldn't forget, unless
I know your being because it is my own.
(But didn't you cry? How I cried.)

Another thing that won't erase—
the howl of face you died with
the look neither soft nor serene—not composed,
the one that knew no gentling—and that unearthly
protesting wail of NOOOOOOOOOOOOOOO
to death—like an animal, my mother said—
the sound I didn't hear
but recognized from her account as mine
years before you came upon your death
as she stood by the couch
you lay on that last time
looking down on you in anguish, in fear—
a sound of monster wind, *chindi*, devil moan,
flung beyond betrayed, betraying breath,
wrung from you as you began to see
that some things can't be denied, turned down.
(Did you think death was a bed,
a stack of dirty dishes,
a stand of roses, petunias,
poppies, cats, dogs, children

you could bulldog to your will?)
Is there not a similar wind, moan, howl, will
in me—placed there by double helix,
their dance and spiral—RNA, DNA—or by
living beside you as I have all my life
until you died, and often enough afterward?
I still ache with desolation
in a similar wind.
(Grandma, what's it like to die?)

Do you suppose that
when grandma dies
more of her stays than goes?

Oakland, 1987

For What Remains Behind

The light was music
flowing from cherry stone to hardwood bud
"like a young girl's dress full of sparkling stones."

In the early morning light the music
fell to the rusty railroad tracks
that run to the mud on the marina.
It accompanied our children as they played "Perils of Pauline,"
hooting diesel sounds as they ran towards the dock.
It was caught in the brilliant kites the morning revellers flew
from the bright grass of the bayside park,
as it carefully jumped over the sidewalk cracks,
as it sprinted stairways into the dark
shadowed windows along the gleaming pastel blocks.

At midday it was madrigal.
It plucked our eyes when we entered a shop
to buy strings of translucent shell that charm a wizard wind
and hold off spirits with their fragile spell.
The late afternoon moon was a jackal sound
revolving the spiked carnival door
into a spiraling round of calliope wind.
We had left old pain behind in the lily-splintered bay
and sang with lips chapped by popcorn and spray.

The night song, mother, was the hush of our meeting.
We'd stayed awake all night, you, Carolee, and I,
while the lights that had caused our city
became as fogbound as the kitchen of our cigarettes.
We talked quietly while the men and children slept,
whispering their pale, salt-washed dreams to the dark.
We waited as shadows must for persons to become,
allowed old anger's witnessing arc
to crumble into ashes and cold coffee grounds.

In the humming kitchen's predawn light
we mouthed old tunes reprising other days,
their tribal songs, and flung our thoughts far from ancestral lines
reprised through ritualless years as lies. In the silence
of those seconds in the newday light, we realized
what we had meant to be. For that small space, mother,
I saw the browning fog fall from your lightstruck eyes.

May 1966

Taking a Visitor to See the Ruins

—for Joe Bruchac

He's still telling about the time he came west
and was visiting me. I knew he
wanted to see some of the things

everybody sees when they're in the wilds of New Mexico.
So when we'd had our morning coffee
after he'd arrived, I said,

Would you like to go see some old Indian ruins?
His eyes brightened with excitement,
he was thinking, no doubt,

of places like the ones he'd known where he came from,
sacred caves filled with falseface masks,
ruins long abandoned, built secure

into the sacred lands; or of pueblos
once home to vanished people but peopled still
by their ghosts, connected still with the bone-old land.

Sure, he said. I'd like that a lot.
Come on, I said, and we got in my car,
drove a few blocks east, toward the towering peaks

of the Sandias. We stopped at a tall
high-security apartment building made of stone,
went up a walk past the pond and pressed the buzzer.

They answered and we went in,
past the empty pool room, past the empty party room,
up five flights in the elevator, down the abandoned hall.

Joe, I said when we'd gotten inside the chic apartment,
I'd like you to meet the old Indian ruins
I promised.

My mother, Mrs. Francis, and my grandmother, Mrs. Gottlieb.
His eyes grew large, and then he laughed
looking shocked at the two

women he'd just met. Silent for a second, they laughed too.
And he's still telling the tale of the old
Indian ruins he visited in New Mexico,

the two who still live pueblo style in high-security dwellings
way up there where the enemy can't reach them
just like in the olden times.

Indian Blood

All I can think about today
is the ways I've been invisiblized,
passed over, turned away, disappeared.
And your eyes, mother, the burning shine
on them, the flame.
Your skin has grown darker
this year of your blood's disease, lupus,
that unacknowledged for so long
in the ignorance of penitence and unspoken
rage, the denial of unshed tears,
dismissal, absence, flight,
turned you away from the roots of your flesh,
the arteries of your life, a disease
that grew within you over the years
untold.
All I can think about is
the resignation of your hands
caught in your lap, words
caught in your throat, vision caught
in your eyes held still, your eyes, your
years, the words now mine
because we share the blood-raged
halfbreed line.
And well I understand the bitter knowledge
of what may not be said, of what
cannot be thought, that grows within our certain
solitude.
I never wanted resignation
for my lot, never would settle
for quiet chores to fulfill my days. I
was too afraid of silence. I was too
weak to imagine a life filled with duty
and unspent memories. I did not have your strength.
Yet tonight I see that you are not
all right, as I have always imagined you to be—
that much is clear in the fevered gaze you fix on me,
fix within yourself, as the old ones have always
done. Your eyes burn dark and bright, your skin
browns, moving to match the earth tones of your

37

inmost soul, your life and your children
dismissed in autumn's flames.
No one can see what
we cannot say.

You keep the picture of my son on your wall,
taken alongside the highway outside
of Laguna when he was six, titled: "Laguna, four
generations away." His blonding hair and
clear, amber eyes gaze out through the window
of the open car door that reflects behind him
the pueblo silent on its rounded hill
along with the camera held in the stranger's hand.
That picture is a measure of our lives: four
generations away from the root of his breath—
your breath, that leaves you in pain.
I wonder what you think when you look at that picture.
Do you remember yourself at that age,
bangs cut straight across your forehead
like Sully's are, Laguna-child style, walking
along the path by the lake with your grandma
on your way to the dances? You say she'd dress up in her
best shawl, black with purple fringe, and say
"Come on, dearie" and taking you by the hand
would begin the trek from New Laguna to Old Laguna.
"And when I'd get tired," you say, "she'd pick me up
and carry me the rest of the way."
You have not forgotten as you are not forgotten
either there or here where the air sits sullen on the hills
and remembers the longago clear crystal sweetness
of stars and shadows, of night.

The hills around Los Angeles are soft
in the evening light. The stars
come out as we speak.
Behind the murderous fog as
when we talk, the words humming between us
like old loves, your voice rippling
like muscles over the wires, "I'm
just putting grandma to bed," you say.
I say what I find myself
wanting to say,
that we must hold to the words we have to share,
hold to our stories, for they are what we have.

The roads are turned to asphalt and their
course is changed, as we have changed
and transformed in the crucible of our lives—you, your children,
your grandchildren, me.
We must each remember everything
that has been said. We must not forget
no matter who turns our stories into lies,
our lives into rubble, our blood
into an enemy that kills.

Halfbreed woman, mother, daughter, sister, wife,
the measure of your blood is of your sight,
your limbs, your knowing that is the same as mine:
you did not forget the charge your grandma laid
on you in fear and rage: "Don't forget you're Indian,"
she said, such few words to guard a woman's life.
She knew how you would be moved away
from the necessities of blood, knew
how lost you would be. But, mama, though you go back
to Laguna only now and then, they
remember you, they remember your name.

Los Angeles, October 1981

Weed

She stood, a weed tall in the sun.
She grew like that and went
over it again and again trying to be tall
trying not to die in the drying sun
the seeming turbulence of waiting
the sun so yellow
so still.

There was nothing else to do. It was like that
in her day, and the sun who rose so bright
so full of fire reminded her of that.
It was the sun that did it; it was the rain.
She stood it all, and more:
the water pounding from the high rock face
of the mesas that made her yard—
she knew where she was growing. Didn't
she know what the sun will do, what happens to weeds
when their growing time's done? Didn't she care?
She got the sun into her, though.
The fire. She drank the rain for fuel.
She stood there in the day, growing,
trying to stand tall like a right weed would.

The drying was part of it.
The dying. Come from heat, the transformation
of fire. The rain helped because it understood
why she just stood there, growing,
tall in the heat and bright.

The old ways go,
tormented in the fires of disease.
My mother's eyes burn,
they tear themselves apart.
Her skin darkens in her fire's heat,
her joints swell to the point
of explosion, eruption.
And oh, the ache: her lungs
don't want to take in more air,
refuse further oxygenation:
in such circumstances,
when volatile substances are intertwined,
when irreconcilable opposites meet,
the crucible and its contents vaporize.

El Cerrito, 1983

Dear World

Mother has lupus.
She says it's a disease
of self-attack.
It's like a mugger broke into your home
and you called the police
and when they came they beat up on you
instead of on your attackers,
she says.

I say that makes sense.
It's in the blood,
in the dynamic.
A halfbreed woman
can hardly do anything else
but attack herself,
her blood attacks itself.
There are historical reasons
for this.

I know you can't make peace
being Indian and white.
They cancel each other out.
Leaving no one in the place.
And somebody's gotta be there,
to take care of the house,
to provide the food.
And that's gotta be the mother.
But if she's gone to war.
If she's beaten and robbed.
If she's attacked by everyone.
Conquered, occupied, destroyed
by her own blood's diverse strains,
its conflicting stains?

Well, world. What's to be done?
We just wait and see
what will happen next.

El Cerrito, 1983

A Piece of Grief, Just a Piece

My mama was a shadow—not
of her former self, she didn't
have a former self—but
a haunt hovering in corners,
hanging around sinks and stoves, known
only by an occasional predictable sniff.

My mama was a shadow, a ghost
in her own life—only she didn't get
a life, taken as it was before her birth
by overkind grandpa, menacing mama,
abusive stepfather, dad who disappeared.
It hurts

to reflect on visits home where she
was all I wanted to see, to share,
someone, something always intervened,
and her
perching here and there, at home
only on the range she loathed
wringing endless dishrags, hiding
in unruffled corner of tightly tidy bed. Oh

she put on a good enough front, fine
furniture, books, paintings, china,
dusted, clean, no dirty dishes in the sink for long,
meals on time entirely unimaginative because
the *real* person, my father,
would not allow creative flow
in his domain. Oh mama, oh

mama. How could you spend so many
years not quite alive in the immaculate cubbies
of your life—those many years unmade

Seal Beach, 1991

sulieaman the aliman the rhythm in my head goes sulieman the allemagne
comen sie heah bitte, that's what they said in Cubero where I was raised
tante Anna tante Eda and the other sister-in-law whose name
I can't remember tante someone on the German side of the family

aunt Anna raised ducks and geese, not the ones Sulieman Ali my son
liked to chase when he was small. she had a pond in dry dry Cubero
in the years of the drought that stretched out a lifetime
and a windmill to finger the wind that Sully never saw

but he saw some of Allemagne, skipping down the Rhine
in his whirly rainbow cap, bitte this, wiedershoen that,
widdershin, veedersayne, auld lang syne how close
the sounds of Gaelic, gallic, Gaul forever undivided are
that no one ever mentioned to my knowledge anywhere

tante Anna's granddaughter Olivia and Teresa my friend and I
would sit in windmill shade and watch the ducks dive in the mud.
at night aunt Anna'd put us to bed in the loft of the madeover barn
become their house when they came to America

if you can call Cubero that, and we slept on featherbeds, under down-filled
comfort and handmade lace-edged sheets just like in Grimm's fairytales
because when they fled they were not allowed to take money, only
what they had converted to goods, but uncle Julius, the fallen away Jew,
died soon after, Anna left with four kids, one of whom is dead this year

the clouds pile over the west mesa, rain puddles on the K-Mart roof. reflecting
on itself, the sky peers down, unmoving, unmoved. all is still except barely
budding boughs of the aging cottonwood tree beyond my sliding glass door,
Star Trek the Next Generation, and the strange sacred heart of Jesus
calendar announcing, "Gurdjieff died for you sins"

reminds me of something I forget—maybe
tante Anna, dead these several years, who doesn't grace our easter table
with her wondrous German cookies anymore. "Du bist Bobby's braut."

her nephew my uncle my mother's last sib or half sib or brother no one
really knows dead last night. he was named Robert Bruce, Robert the Bruce.
oh where and oh where is my highland laddie gone from el rancho gallito—
se fue. there is less and less there here.

and more and more of there here wherever it is we are.
wherever you go, there you are, the bumper sticker proclaims, verdad, so it
occurs that the dead must be wherever it is they are (were) (have been)
(will be) forever and ever amen

when I was small Bobby the Bruce was engaged to my dad's sister Izzy
from the Lebanese side of the family, and tante Anna used to say when she
saw Izzy who was the youngest daughter and taught me to walk
or was that aunt Ada another daughter

taught me to recite nursery rhymes, the Gettysburg Address,
back in the wartime when I was barely two? I've been to Gettysburg where the
murdered horses still scream. Hans, Anna's elder son,
taught me to waltz new year's 1944 when he was home on leave.

who taught Anna to say to Izzy "Du bist Bobby's braut" longlongago
back in the village near Kaiserslautern on the Rhine where I went
years after she died before Bobby, Kurt, Mama, Ookie the Sid did

our Jewish Indian hero and his braut didn't marry after all. cancelled the
wedding when he returned from occupying Japan after the Bomb twenty
years old even though he had brought a whole set of china from there,

and I suppose, radioactivity, though no one even mentioned that. later he
married a local girl, sister-in-law of Jido's best friend Dave Armijo of the west
mesa land grant where all those Anglos live. Dave died years before Jido died
soon after he saw Sulieman thought his son's son's son was born, forgot or
never knew Sully's brother Fuad my heart was dead

Jido got mixed up a lot by then. Bob and his other braut wed in grandma's
garden on the Laguna/Scottish side, next to the lily pond, on the green lawn
near the arbor groaning beneath the weight of bridal wreath, beneath the
weeping willow tree, weep for me, and someone sang love songs the names I
can't remember

but I remember the songs, the ladies in filmy huge brimmed hats, a garden
party in Cubero where a Jewish Indian married a lost daughter of the Armijo
family from the old New Mexican side of the family.

in Cubero outsiders make a strange clan, connected by blood, proximity,
shared events, history, fate. comadre, compadre, primo, amte, guwatze, how
are you and oiga! que pasa, qu'estas'ciendo, dude! Odd sounds and tones that

later made me sing to Sully the boy of wilderness, Solomon the wordy wise
who must have brought me to it though he could not speak
for I've not made funny punny word-song lullabies before or since
except for some strange reason just today.

anyway Bobby had horses, windmills, great earthen dams and steel tanks
where I learned to swim, and real estate in Cibola County the fabled land
everyone travelled to find back in the times before history came out west to
find goldless people already here

Izzy had kids, jazz, and a steakhouse in the Big Q
and golf widowhood which was practice for the real thing,
and keeping books like she learned in Cubero when I was two and three

and everyone would never die, and keeping up with the family—
the one on the Lebanese side, the one on the Italian side,
fixing homemade pizza and kibbe, buchilato, biscochitos, marmoul,
apple pie, corresponding with her once upon a time these years.

last time I saw Isabel was the day Wendy on the Lebanese side though his
father was German American from somewhere in the east died too young
no, at her birthday when pop picked a fight with the dude serving us. today
uncle's gone, aunt's widowed for I can't remember how many years.

tante Anna's son Kurt died a year or so ago, my mom the year before,
granddaddy her immigrant German stepfather years ago about the time
my daughter was born from the Lebanese side of the family until I was forced
to flee to the Big Q for her life and mine from Grants, Cibola County
where all the gold was yellowcake, glowed in the dark

and on our skin like pollen upon butterfly winds, from whence I fled
and now most of that part of the family is dead and I'm a widow, a gay divorcee
getting older, glowing more and more like plastic Mary I had in the fifties
when I was young and only one or two had died and I'd never been to a
funeral and the apple tree was still alive.

ash wednesday's coming on ashes to ashes, dust to dust
not in tante Anna's peaked roof barn of a house she kept
over all the years, tending its vegetable garden just out the back door
an outhouse for a toilet because she thought it belonged outside
with the windmill, the ducks & geese, the pond.

at her funeral in the Big Q the strange minister praying over her Lutheran
remains told god about Anna the sinful so he would forgive. I grinned—I
couldn't help it and no one could see—a woman lost thousands of miles from
her Rhineland village, Christian braut of a Jew who fled into the desert
of mesas, hovering peaks, eternal sky

in all those years in the Cubero of her life never learned English or Spanish
so couldn't speak except to her kids. imagine tante Anna sinning
speechless, standing at the stove while pleasing Satan with beating
sugared butter into fine flour to feed the family the world on Easter day

sulieman the allemand, sulieman ali the man who writes buttery
tales of sinless grins, greets people "Grossgott!" with satirical salute
fist pounded against brow left foot stamping loud the floor the ground
and never sins and isn't dead like the spring,

like his tiny brother all these years is dead
one of my earliest loves to go and leave me here
or Bobby Shaftoe who went to see, to sea, after an attack, last night

no association is ever free

lucky lucky Bobby. lucky lucky Anna. lucky lucky ma. Lurt, Gene Lebanese
the conquistador from Mora whose last name in English means black snake.
grandma. Ookie the Sid. Johnny Canzoneri of steaks and jazz.

Fuad whose name means my heart. granddaddy, German immigrant who
fought the Kaiser and his own brother in the first world war. uncle Lee
Hanosh sang Lebanese high-songs in Arabic the wondrous at christenings and
weddings and his brother Joe played the derbukke
I haven't heard since Amo died

and primo Wendy dead with Jido, Sitte, Haula, Zahia, Josephine, Pauline,
everyone except Naphie the oldest daughter on the Lebanese side,
Izzy, Ada, Liás—spelled elias but everyone here says it wrong, my dad
on the living side, Cecil

Rose Fidel who was hardly that, Hanna, her husband big black snake. say no
ill of the dead which is almost everyone I used to know when I was young,
and dead was something only grandmas did, Mina my dad's mom, Sitte,
grandma Gunn on the Laguna side. now everyone goes into the arroyo, onto
the faraway sea including Cubero, the sweet water spring, the apple tree

kifik. grossgott. everyone. and synce ye're gaun, vaya con dios.
tante Anna and Bob the Bruce's family's name was Gottlieb
god dear or maybe dear god.
saalem u khalem, du-wih shatz, mine schatz

Albuquerque, 1994

Myth/Telling – Dream/Showing

1.

so where do we go next?
(into sunrise)

2.

there is all the clutter:
on the walls, the table top,
in the sink, all over the counters,
on the stove, the sofa, the floors.

3.

the bird, yellow, green and blue
who lives in a cage with an open door
chirps now and then. drops onto the table
for breakfast.

4.

the cloud in the north, she said.
she meant the united states.

5.

I don't care, he said. I love
the united states. it isn't fair.
I never killed any indians. I am not
responsible for what my ancestors did.
I love the wilderness, he said. the indians
can't keep me out of it.

6.

and then there's the indian woman
who hates in herself what is white.
says she sees it like vomit. like
a crippled withered leg she must drag
with her everywhere she goes.

7.

and there is all the litter. the hours
passing. the exhaustion. the cloud
that is what I have to do today. not
go to the water. not go to the mesa.
go into the city. the cloud.

8.

the indian woman is cursed with lupus.
a blood disease. in which your blood
devours you.

9.

the white man goes to yosemite
on vacation. it's his recreation.
yes, says another man, black. it's
your recreation, but it's their life.

10.

the north of here is oregon, washington.
mt. st. helen's. that cloud.

11.

the bird dreams in his cage.
about lunch. he doesn't dream of trees.
he never saw one, doesn't know what they are.

12.

I have to put my feathers on.
go through the door that opens.
into wilderness. city traffic.
bird-empty streets.

13.

if dawn comes (if corn comes).
if it is sunrise. that soft and blessing.
where someone is going, next.
if spring comes. (summer-people time.)
corn-is-growing time.
where/when-someone-is-going-next time.

Runes

1.

out today
imagining rainbows
surf high and tangly
winter tide
stirs things up
healing.
storm out there
up north somewhere.
gulls sheer off course
incisively.
intent
like child gaze
a certain quality of still
slowly surrounds

2.

chocolate soldier
aromatic   deep
a quiet comfort
for days that melt
slowly into dark swirls
like this: like this:
like that.
stirred   and melted
poured   and moulded
sculptured sweetness
but   strong
memory of song
of stone

3.

it's the holes
that are hardest to understand
how they came to be
how they are never
filled
dark mystery and volumes
of no words
just there   something
missing, missed,
skies are holes
and stars.
there are holes in me.
a ragman
tattering.

4.

somehow the brightness was wounded
and what had been meant for shadow
was playing in the sun
a quirk of lunation, precession

zodiacal turns not taken fully
into account and negative space
understood positively

a gestalt. the foreground
flickering behind, the background
brilliant before. and all around
a teetering, a wavering, thin
in the crystalline air

or as voices spun into light
a harmony, melody belied,
dark in the place of light,
memory in the place of reason,
sun in the place of stars

an awkward occasion, then.
something simple, direct,
misapplied, plunged into meaning,
i regret that i could not utter
what was in me to say
it was a blade
incision
a forever opened vein

5.

into emptiness step
and lowering
into darkness go
high hero with stetson and rifle pause
on a mesa etch ebon
brilliant dying sky
step at last
beyond sight
disappear

6.

knife under bed
will slice the pain in two
blade between boards
will sever any connections
today the black and vital carpenter
came to my house
instructing in construction
blew painful not high overhead
sailed right by me
carried on the wings of mosquito
hawk stuck somehow behind
the couch and left dust
over the manuscripts and the tools
blew out the lights re
constructing some ancient
magnificence   sought
in handbooks and dusty kits

7.

on a day like any other
except for erratic blossoms
a smiling deep on the wind
falling around head and shoulders
gently murmuring their way
to the ground to wink out
like new snow.
they were also white.
and except for a sound
the butterflies winging
the petal fall
a misty niagara
floating
in the space between
and a certain glance
piling up inside as quiet
as the snow

8.

it's also hard to understand
how missing a song not ever
heard (not remembered, anyway)
can lead to breath-held—
unutterable, a tightness
in the throat
longing for a soaring note
an arching of tone pure
and sudden *bel*
graceful *canto* up
into arched heights that lead
voice and instrument
into clear

such things left over
from dream, maybe, but
when recognized that tightness
the only clue that could be traced
(I suppose) spiraling on a smoky track
in the furthest source
but trackers have clear notions
of where to go

9.

splintering
an enterprise
of sorcerers
awkward with elbows
they writhe
hopping between cobwebbed
spells and gargoyle tunes
sounding among stone walls
begin in spider-shadows
to sing

in careful corners
of unadulterated thought
hair of frog
eye of newt
muttering and rubbing
hands grow slowly sere
a mist rises to fill the room
ancient eyes peer forth
intently.

10.

remembering shadows from years
gone by the darkness entering
just after the light the
seamless words of entropy
a saturnian thing that walked
the streets crying:
didn't recognize the friends
from other times but knew
enough to come in from the rain.
the book that used to haunt my shelves
now too is gone. followed,
I suppose, the mind sent off
in the mail long ago
forgot to put a return address
on the envelope. was always
forgetting things like that.

11.

dry rustling
ever so slightly
leaves move
dry and dusty
in the early autumn light
a lizard creeps forth
mumbling quietly
tongue flicks in and out
tasting testing
air dries in the sun
muttering

12.

axiomatic.
aromatic.
automatic.
centuries bloom.
wither on bent branches
a piney wood
a trickle of stream
growing
going down to sea.
can be tracked
by word
of mouth:
inclination.

13.

a folded chair
litter of blankets
coffee drunk and cold
last night's ashes
wet and empty
hearth whose home was cupped
in careful sentences in careless wiles
twining. braided like runes
this significance
mosaic, angles, bits of light
unpatterning
a whir of wings
shattering

14.

there's a starburst pattern on the ceiling
above the bed, above the eye of regard,
in answer to a question unasked
quietly, in that gloom gleaming
a certain peripatetic look

around this a floor
bursting with stars of its own
below the window, below the mind of entering,
a question suggested
inserted guilessly
all the while
nudges

15.

bits of light strewn about the floor like rushes
idly the woman sweeps straw from hair
wishes for gold and deliverance
arranges skirt and body in a single sigh
sits at last at wheel
tears fall over scanty light
remembering the price of ransom
and the promised sun
she spun gold from rage and terror
lost in the splices
of rumplestiltskin days
promise of redemption

16.

in beauty built
with beauty blest
in beauty wrought
with beauty felt
the beauty tasted
the light unmet
the gold
the bright
remember
do not let fall
the sacrifice
do not that beauty
stay
but carefully
while light still splatters
like ineradicable ink on the splintered floor
recalls

17.

walking on water
isn't too difficult
there is a certain
spider does it all the time
(plane and angle to be properly
applied)
it's what he said
the surface tension
creates its own momentum
making many things
possible

18.

enclosing space
limiting limits
tight and lidded
eyes go forth
not in song
in perpetuity
boxes dry and dusty
glittering and rare
smoldering in memory
a lostlong time
parameters defined
frozen
in light

19.

the light I feel when
a certain connection is made
falls silent in the emptiness
of between
and lies waiting

a small secret.

I hide carefully that light
made necessary by circumstance
a circling brightness like
some rambling angel
gets lost in the streets
of alliance
of blood

it's there though
whenever called—along
with other things

in deep caverns beneath my feet
drums sound

a continent awash in blood
babies splattered against cave walls
where the people ran to hide
or had been herded by the white men
with guns
it's how the west was won

I remember the pity of the one who cried
as he blew my baby's head off
merciful moments before
my turn came

20.

and then there is the confusion
a kind of deafness that troubles
the mind making moves toward
hearing what has been said
appear like mole-groping
in the dark

and over the centuries this
is understandable even though
one must wonder why.

enjoyment does not come easily
to one who has had each pleasure
snatched before half through
which leads in the end to numbness
to tunneling for safety, avoiding

21.

caught in a tooth
trying to jog it
loose tongue
applied selectively
probing for that moment
in exactitude
allowing full flickering
a perfect similitude
like silence which passes
in the dark for trains

22.

frozen
the figure stands
startled
rifle stretches space
just at the moment of raised

infinity mirrors
that gaze
stopped between
image

and what's forgot
behind eyes something moves apart
lets sudden space
come in

what is willed
becomes law
inevitability
pursues him

the stripped Mother's
breast cries vengeance
breath binds spell
raised arm not quite

bowed
at the just recovered shrine
not yet enacted
this rite

23.

eye of spring
a tension of surfaces
mathematicians delight
drowsing in sun those
coils of light and shade
cool and bright
such splatterings as drops
of sunlight on water make
that precision that can be
set down in its entirety
by those who manipulate
such orders, ordinal,
cardinal, integer, faction,
direction taken. ready, aim,
a focus of combination
with understanding
ratio cination
and written down in graceful
equation a certain balance
proved: y'all come outta there
with yer hands up

24.

clear and cold the waters
rise from the spring at the foot
of the mountain
in such times
the air is sweet
and free

in the cycles of the heart
such times come and go
filling
arising
true as emptiness
as failure

splendor pulled from earth
compelled to admit
towering mountain
with his last breath
name her aright
if for the first time.

stunned
enchantment holds
his tongue—
patience.
it is not yet time
to drink.

25.

fractured
head plate in pieces
through which light
softly makes its presence known

if you should stoop
and pick up one small fragment
place it to your head
you will see how
all the pieces fit

26.

in the last analysis
whatever matters will
come to light
entwined with intent
combined with memory
and alight on edge
of table or desk
wait patiently for notice—
an image here, a line there,
slowly building, structure
on structure, wire here
switch there
careful connection awaiting
recognition: the law of soldiering
decreed by generals
a hundred years before
"nits breed lice"

27.

memory matters
like hydrogen
when specifically
combined
falls and arises
resurrection a
daily occurrence
watch the sky
for omens por
tentious occasion
arise with abso
lute predictability
with proper sigh ting
align
in all reason to de
clare that careful
construction will
drop and splinter
later disappear
"they never lived here
anyway
only their memories"

28.

the moon is a signal
key   what the old
witch doctor said
that shattering
fracturing of grammar
that understanding a
line thrown out of century
light source battery
going unrecognized
omens misread because
telling time by the light
of the moon is the differential
a variable of slight acquaintance
deflected over generations
genes misapplied and learning
lessons based on nonsequitur
(nonsequentiality, a random
that is truly so) cannot be
learned

29.

words caught just
at threshold of utterance
sound choked off before
mind has time to think
delaying
holding
back integrity
a certain flowering
stopped

thought in circles sniffing scent
(a lonely dog seeking the moon,
a familiar scent to follow)
vanished into thin air
unspoken   birds
silently move into the darkening sky
along the waterways
angling   hunter wades
surrounded in plaintive air
strains of old music arouse the ear
in time the moon/ shines clear

30.

I have thought about ladders
and two-way streets
and making change overthecounter
value given for value bought
and entropy
and silence
the fading edge of hope
frayed like the edge of an old slip
taken down in half light
but no metaphor reaches
beyond the darkened corners of the room
no vision will restore the dead
no lie will twist what is so to be otherwise

but oh I wish I knew who it is to be alive
to be able to simply recognize
the horror embedded in memory
waiting patiently
but realizing makes such pain in me
no easy matter—to simply write
what happens now, or then. it is
beyond me on ordinary days
to acknowledge what I know
and what I see. I was carefully
constructed to forget what is
before my eyes. the conqueror teaches that, you know.
so we will never say what is so.
so no one will ever know.

San Francisco, March 1981

Grandmother

Out of her own body she pushed
silver thread, light, air
and carried it carefully on the dark, flying
where nothing moved.

Out of her body she extruded
shining wire, life, and wove the light
on the void.

From beyond time,
beyond oak trees and bright clear water flow,
she was given the work of weaving the strands
of her body, her pain, her vision
into creation, and the gift of having created,
to disappear.

After her,
the women and the men weave blankets into tales of life,
memories of light and ladders,
infinity-eyes, and rain.
After her I sit on my laddered rain-bearing rug
and mend the tear with string.

Molly Brant, Iroquois Matron, Speaks

I was, Sir, born of Indian parents, and lived while a child among
those whom you are pleased to call savages; I was afterwards sent to live
among the white people, and educated at one of your schools; and after
every exertion to divest myself of prejudice, I am obliged to give my
opinion in favor of my own people. . . . In the government you call
civilized, the happiness of the people is constantly sacrificed to the
splendor of empire. . . .

—Joseph Brant

We knew it was the end
long after it had ended,
my brother Joseph and I.
We were so simple then,
taking a holiday to see the war,
the one they would later call
the Revolution.
The shot sent 'round the world
was fired from the Iroquois gun; we
could not foresee its round
would lodge itself
in our breast. The fury we unleashed
in pursuit of the Great Peace
washed the Mothers away,
our Longhouses burned,
our fields salted,
our ancient Fires extinguished—
no, not put out, fanned,
the flames spread far
beyond our anticipation,
out of control.
We had not counted on their hate;
we had not recognized
the depth of their contempt.
How could we know I would be
no longer honored matron
but heathen squaw,
in their eyes, my beloved daughters
half-breed dirt. Along with our earth
they salted our hearts

so nothing would grow
for too long a time.
We had been arrogant
and unwise: engaged in spreading
the White Roots of Peace, we
all but forgot the little ones
dear to our clan Matrons
and their ancestry,
the tender fortunes
of squash, corn and beans.

Then, overnight, was I
fleeing for my life
across the new borders, my brother hunted
like a common criminal
to be tried for sedition
for his part
among the British. They
lost out just as we'd planned
a century before. But
we had forgotten the Elders' Plan.
So it was we could not know
a Council Fire would be out,
the League unable to meet
in the bitter winter that fell
upon us like the soldiers
and the missionaries,
the carrion birds that flew
upon the winds of revolution
to feed upon our scarred and frozen flesh.
We had not counted on fate—
so far from the roots of our being
had we flown,
carried on the wings of an Algonquin priest
we fell into the eyrie
of a carrion host.
Perhaps it is the Immortals alone who know
what turns the revolution must entail,
what dreams to send to lead us on,
far beyond the borders of our Dreams.
The turning of centuries goes on,
revolving along some obscure path
no human woman's ever seen.

That's how it is with revolutions.
Wheels turn. So do planets.
Stars turn. So do galaxies.
Mortals see only this lifetime
or that. How could we know,
bound to the borders we called home,
the revolution we conspired for
would turn us under
like last year's crop?

I speak now because I know
the revolution has not let up.
Others like my brother and like me
conspire with other Dreams,
argue whether or not
to blow Earth up, or poison it mortally,
or settle for an alteration. They
believe, like we, that the sacred fire
is theirs to control, but maybe
this revolution is the plan of gods,
of beings Matrons and priests alike
cannot know.

Still, let them obliterate it, I say.
What do I care? What have I to lose,
having lost all I loved so long ago?
Aliens, aliens everywhere,
and so few of the People
left to dream. All that is left
is not so precious after all—
great cities, piling drifting clouds
of burning death, waters that last drew breath
decades, perhaps centuries ago,
four-leggeds, wingeds, reptiles all
drowned in bloodred rivers of an alien dream
of progress. Progress is what
they call it. I call it cemetery,
charnel house, soul sickness,
artificial mockery
of what we called life.

I, Matron of the Longhouse, say:
If their death is in the fire's wind,
let it wash our Mother clean.

If revolution is to take another turn,
who's to say
which side will turn up next?
Maybe when the last great blast goes up
you will hear me screaming with glee,
wildly drunk at last on vindication,
trilling ecstatically my longed-for revenge

in the searing unearthly wind.

Elegy for My Son

I wanted to write 1968 for today's date—as though
somewhere between then and
then, some step taken could be untaken, or a word
spoken be unsaid
some little thing done
not
wouldn't lead into
where with bewildered hands I sit
holding your small body dead.

Iroquois Sunday: Watertown, 1982

"If it doesn't make awareness higher,
it isn't art," he said, that Indian
from Ottowa. He'd come all the way
for the powwow. To sell some pictures
and carvings he'd made. "You see
the serpent, the woman, the man. You know
what Freud says about serpents," he said
to my white friend, staring at her the way
men do at women. She knew. Moved uneasy,
angry, away. She told me about it
later, after we left and went to the
Dairy Queen in town for a bite to eat.
He'd shown us his pictures, discoursing
on the nature of true art. One of them
was of two tree stumps that had a few
branches rising slender toward the sky.
If you looked at it just right you could see
an eagle hovering, wings pointed down,
over two heads, the man's looking up and out,
the woman's lowered, humbly behind. He
pointed that out, or you wouldn't have known
one was a man's, one was a woman's.

"What kind of Indian are you?" I asked.
He didn't say, but I know. Coyote Indian.
There was a big stone grinding wheel
mounted on a stand. The children played
with it all afternoon. The powwow was at
one of the women's houses
that was built on a suburban plot.
It was made of logs. Sitting
on the front steps, we watched the clouds.
The children tumbled in the grass like raccoons.
When it began to rain, everyone went inside.
Sat around, talking, watching the children
play. The men wandered from room to room.

They played poker with the Tarot cards.
The women watched the corn soup boiling,
the coffee dripping into the Pyrex pot,

the hot scones browning. Those women
don't talk to eagles. They talk to snakes.
To the grandmothers. They tell fortunes
with the cards. They read omens
beneath the sky. They count raindrops
in time to every latest craze. They survive,
grinding axes, teeth, fingers and minds
sharp as blades.

Suiciding(ed) Indian Women

Koyukan

broken a
tremble like
windowpane in gusted
wind I envision you
Koyukan
on the southern shore writing
stepping slowly in the circle
as traditional in your view
as Wolverine in any metropolis
but your shaken voice,
is it a small wind we carry
in our genes, fear of disappearance?
an utterance that hovers
at the edges of our lips, forever
left unsaid? The stories
around Laguna say that Iyetiku
left the people longtimeago.
There was a drought.
She gave them some toys
for gambling, you know, but the men
gambled everything, no matter how
their sisters pleaded
or even their aunts
and hid in the kivas
so the women couldn't nag
and they wouldn't even do
the necessary dancing.
So Iyetiku got mad
and went away. That's what
the story says, anyway, and maybe
it's so. Maybe she knew that we
could do without her presence
in the flesh, and she left Iarriku—
the perfect ear of corn
to remind men that she was near,
to honor women, the woman
in the earth, and in themselves.

So they call themselves her name,
call themselves Mother,
or maybe they sent her away
and made up the rest.

Laguna

small woman huddled on the couch
soft light and shadows try to comfort you
Laguna would-be suicide
why do you cling to the vanished lake?
The water has left the village.
You hardly speak except to say
confusion fills your mind.
How can you escape the ties
of brutaldrunken father
gossipy sisters/aunts
scolding uncles/brothers
who want you to buy and
cook their food
you eat little yourself
you say. Why must
you in your strongtoothed beauty
huddle helpless on the edge
laugh mocking your own terrible
pain, why are things so rotten
that you can't see another world
around you like the lamps
soft and comforting
around this room?

Navajo

earthwoman
authentic as any whiteman
could wish you marry out
and unhappy you brown
and laughing, your flowing
hair, Navajo, you can't
understand why squawman
sits in a chair, orders
you and your young sisters
you knew the reservation
was no place to be

you giggle about the anguish
of your past the men your
mother married it will not
be like that for you
and you know it must
unless you get away
but how divide yourself
from your flesh? Division
does not come easy
it is against the tribe,
laws which only few honor.
Nor do you understand why
as you hold your uneasy perch
on the edge and make joking
memories do for real.

Shipap

Beautiful Corn Woman
lost all these ages ago
stolen as your children
for generations have been
and it is not right
that this should be
but the law is such
they abandoned you
defied the women
gambled and lost
and you left them
they don't tell how
they put women
out of the sacrfice
except in your emblem—
and death and
destruction
have followed them.
The people lost
the beautiful first home
to the raging war gods
and wander homeless now.
They have taken your name.

Teaching Poetry at Votech High, Santa Fe, The Week John Lennon Was Shot

I

Crepe paper Christmas
green and red, turns
and twists, symmetrical,
around the partitioned
segments of the barnsized room—
voices of brown and white young,
rejects from more hallowed halls
on their way to factories in some
nameless and partitioned open space
in the unbending world
of their faceless fate—blend with
mechanical and electronic chatter.
Noise everywhere, scrambling over
untouched books glossy and slick
with disuse. A groan and clatter
of highmigraine screech pulses
unidentified, predictable,
sets my teeth on edge.
My brainends turn, twist,
try to tune themselves
to unpredictability,
to something textured,
recognizable. Still,
I inhabit this slick universe:
hired to teach glossy poetry.
Through their eyes,
I see myself punitive, demanding, irrelevant.
Though I am not
vocationally authorized,
I hold the chalk.

Electronic mornings creep
over my horizon,
fill my days with danger, hang
ominous over the Rio Grande,
chase the mesas north.
On the highway early
driving north from Albuquerque
I saw sunrise gold and dayglopink billow
on the smoke of the electric plant

outside of Bernalillo.
So much beauty in the certain destruction
it spewed into the December crystal air.
Winter settling on the land, a nestling bird.
Stalks of winter-frosted grass
pointed to me my way, made
my pathway clear.
Last night on the late news
they announced John Lennon's murder,
said he died climbing the stairs.
Remembering when I
was on the other side of the desk,
the twenty years between,
I wept.
How had we come to this?
The shots that took him down
spewed a strawberry trail on the steps,
the blood washed away just after
by the city's rain.

II

The best of the world
slumps before me in the room—
minds that eighteen years ago
first turned earthward blinking:
oh yeah.
Wasted.
Turned off.
Tuned in to video narcosis,
stereophonic shuddering light,
in which, transfixed,
these naked angels burn, golden pink,
their hopes and mine on dust and booze.
They smirk about "Ever Clear,"
explain when I ask
that it's 180 proof alcohol
unaware of the implications in the name,
of what
another time
the words might mean—
or perhaps not unaware.
There is a certain glint
on each institution-frosted face.
They have grown,

unawares, into electronic commodities,
haven't the will to fight
the mindless nothing that infuses
inexorable anguish into their lives.
Stoned like martyrs of their ancient faith
they go down their days
not understanding
how they've been crucified,
or by who,
they make do with plastic reveries sunk
in heedless desperation.
Synthetic clatter crusts
their days, makes electro-
chemical tissue of their gaze.

What world is this?
Cut off, torn away, shattered, maybe
they dream of when it will get better,
of when they will be free.

III

180 proof.
Neither womb nor honest texture provides
rough comfort or sure throbbing grasp.
Quivering, these desperados
hide beneath sham and sneer,
behind closed eyes, disheveled hair,
stoned on chemicals and beer.
What do they become, these children,
the same age as my own,
who I watch staggering into life,
despair rising
brown and stinking within their eyes
like poison on the desert air?
It billows gold and pink
around their faces, their helpless heads:
They do not plan, they do not dream.
There is no future they can bear.
I want to cradle them,
murmur to keep them from knowing
what I fear.
I will not let them see me weep.
I will fight with them instead,
sneer and rage.
Tell them to be quiet, to sit down.

IV

No munchkin voices. An English
sharpwood point breaks with a smug tap.
Muffled sounds rise in my ears,
the bite of lemon fills my nostrils.
They pass it around, juice sticking
to their hands. I am surrounded
by eyes that canny and closed
measure me, gaze surreptitiously
from faces no more than
nineteen years old.
Artificiality-induced
boredom barely masks
their scorn of the dusty
plastic tiempo their minds are frozen in;
barely differentiated into carpets,
chalkboards, partitions,
desks, shelves, jackets, slacks,
glossy animal posters on the walls.
They understand
the nature of their punishment.
They do not understand their crimes.
They sit behind plastic faces
barely differentiated into closed
and empty, resentful and dazed. They
are sick with disuse,
plasticized in atrophic rage.

V

Touch skin:
one's own
dewy with petrochemicals
soft for now.
Remember wood
gleaming and warm
accepting you—
smells and oils,
polishing.
Handle plastic
that refuses to recognize
whatever it is you are,
huddled into petrochemical clothing
acrylic
cold

unrewarding
no energy in it.
Know the exact dimension
of a dying soul.

VI

Tired.
Week nearly done.
Mind a tree,
peeling dead bark
littering the ground,
waiting
for the last molecule
to be released.
This rubble of ash
shaped into glazed and battered blocks
forms the walls, gray because they are
held together by despair.
Roughshod voices ride
the lockerlined metalclang corridor.
Eyes glitter on the brink
of suicide.
The principal stalks the lateday halls
the tiny snackbar beyond the farther door.
He collars those who loiter
in these dispirited halls,
haranguing, ordering. His brown face
looks siempre tired.
His familiar Chicano body sags slightly
into his next word. He knows
what he sees. His limp loose tie
bespeaks discouragement, fatigue.
The students allow his harsh
ministrations, pretend to obey
until he is out of sight down the hall,
then return to loitering,
neck halfheartedly, play pinball
on a slightly sagging machine.
Two o'clock.
Ten more minutes and I'll be free.

I teach the students lost
to plastic rugs and desks,

watch silty minds
grainy to my thought's touch
ooze helpless to the glazed acrylic floor.
Before me one young face
reflected in hand-held glass
gleams.

VII

Wood   steel   over emotional   motivation   sullen
firetaste   smoke   harsh hash   herbs gross green
bitter   lemonpeel   coffeegrounds awful   seeds
like wood burning   nutcrust   walnutskin goats
milk   the aftertaste   liquidy resin   kumquats
sour cherries   sharp   a tar burn   tongues fire
stream chill flight   harpoon   spiraling   tight
grapefruit tangy   bite spaced   torn from shoots
green apricots   sour blackberries   grogged air
kind of asleep   stomach hurt   chest sorry   full
tingle muscle   pulse   pulse   pulse   speed to
flight adrenalin spike taking off   meadows rise
in pleasuring thick as sour cream rancid cheese
fresh milk from fat dusty cows   taste of blood
coats warm throat what do we do with the hole
that's left   staggering   bleeding on the steps
ripe   ripped   on the powered air   stale burning
rising incense nicotine sweet   fingers nauseous
air content   powdered sugar hills   stiff grass
pointing billowing into the blood the pain a mom
ent   only   gone fish   ride   lakes na'more clear
defined   strawberry place rising   a stair   plas
tic fields silent   time grows in cement cracks
soft fiber fall   a feather of breath   lemon air

VIII

Around me
the faces are forests
retreating into snow they
whisper about taking her down
giggle defiance . eyes
prepared for punishment
because they KNOW, in carnality
(¡oigan! ¡carnales!)
My words fall on history-reddened ears

She? / He? Who is it that speaks?
"See, man—I mean ma'am (smirk)
You know HE'S talking to HER
because the Beatles are male, man,
and HE says:
let me take you down"
(leering at the thought).
(Dying at the shot, yeah, man,
he's been taken down, *verdad*.)
They do not mention the tone of grief.

Winter here. We wish for spring.
For ease maybe somewhere
for running across fields
forever alive forever free
in some packaged plastic freeze-
dried recurrent fantasy.
But red with the ridicule of self-abuse
in front of me their postures are
vaguely fused to the carmine blaze of rage
that right to the quick bites deep,
touches me in that secret place
where no one dares to go, not even me,
though I KNOW
that inward lifelong sentence, that
single thought that holds
a life in matter's field,
that now bruised and icy bleeds
sweet juice red as ripe berries
on the forever frozen grass

IX

The noise and clutter
of each separate day
fuses into sound:
learned in grit
in multidecible shriek, we
learned to say what there is to say
under bricks, under rubble of dead
elephants' dream
transformed into heaps of ivory
hedge against inflation
learned that daddy won't come home

he was never there anyway
to take it step by step
like one child stepped
(how many years ago)
trying to get home
scrambling among words
groping for comprehension
among the sneers alongside the tears,
cut off in the smoke of winter air—
and life and a not necessary death
sufficient for that time—still, quiet, dead.

Later that day it rained.

Affirmation

—for Andrew Salkey

Imperceptible
the forest stands
within the boughs unnoticed
undeclared
moving as the light
the wind
plays the eternal game:
manifestation.

So, grandmothers,
your gifts still go with me
unseen.
To reach.
Slowly
to go
(as the tree makes its way through the earth)
the simultaneous thought of this
and other
makes the distance between each point disappear.

So mornings rise above the trees. Wind
sings night's ache away. The terrors
(small learned-psychotic bursts) fade
beyond the great living star that warms our thoughts
(my
thought
you
the forest
inexorable
there
each making)

Small things count after all:
each leaf a tale,
each journey retracing some ancient myth
told in shadows and whispers
under the flickering boughs:
sacred making (sacrificing).
The power of Spider thoughts
so small
mount, thread by thread.

The oracle says, *go south (enter vastness)*
persevere.
The sunlight falls through the trees, illuminating
hidden paths. Grandmother
slips just beyond sight, for one
instant stands clear in the sunlight
on the edge of the path,
disappears.

The rivers are still mighty.
Midnight tells each star its place.
We do not count the drops,
the moving
each and each,
but every turning, imaged in its dark surprise,
moves its own way
as we are moved
never knowing just why we came,
or on what morning,
how.

Powwow 79, Durango

haven't been to one in almost three years
there's six drums and 200 dancers a few
booths piled with jewelry and powwow stuff
some pottery and oven bread
everyone gathers
stands for the grand entry
two flag songs
and the opening prayer by some guy
works for the BIA
who asks our father
to bless our cars
to heal our hearts
to let the music here tonight
make us better, cool
hurts and unease
in his son's name, amen.
my daughter arrives, stoned,
brown face ashy from the weed,
there's no toilet paper
in the ladies room she accuses me
there's never any toilet paper
in the *ladies* room at a powwow she glares
changes
calms
it's like being home after a long time

Tucson: First Night

the stars.
softness on the brutal land.
the song.
rest here. the reflective
pause (deflection)
what things we do, being
(hands like butterflies in July evening sun) I recall
water calling down the tender grass,
the moment hovers.
do I say clouds? see how they piled
over the sandstone mesas
that made one boundary of my home
(the land is central to this)
focused or unfocused
eyes formed shapes to be dissolved
saw time finally an illusion
carved out of rock, motion, a word put
upon the wind: the road
was the other boundary. the highway
went around us before I was born,
motion elliptical as the thought I took,
moving away until found, it holds. "The Road," we said,
like Plato in our innocence
like nothing would ever be
different, rhythms ever the same:
and so it is.
clouds that were there
are here. now. my mind and the sky
one thing on the edge of surmise (sunrise).

I travel a lot these days:
Albuquerque,
San Francisco,
Los Angeles,
New York,
Nova Scotia,
London,
San Diego.
Sometimes I don't know which place is this,
what year, like in this desert resort
where cactus lines the walks

and the blue lit pool is still;
where expensive people walk by
and soft November air breathes warm upon my shoulders
benediction
sign of home
voices of friends scattered all over
the moon hanging low in the sky
bottom curve lit, looking pregnant. the last
week before the descent, and this night: dry
and candles in the bar, shrill and soft
voices around us ignored.
We look out at the patio, Tucson lights
bright below. You show me my childhood,
etching memories—making things
emerge. Strange to sit in a strange city
beside a man I met years ago somewhere else
and haven't seen since, a passing
acquaintance passing me over to my past,
unreal in all its dimensions, familiar, loved—

There is the history:
in the papers, 2 Acoma youths accused of killing
a state cop, in the courts, tried, convicted, appealed
(*Indians believe in witchcraft*
the expert ethnologist says).
In the fiction, *they exorcised a brujo, they*
killed a son of a bitch, on the people's tongues—
especially on the tongues—*Willie was*
never any good anyway, he broke his parents' hearts—
how many stories, which makes which history true?
Hero becomes villain, villain fool—and
what about Willie Fillipe?
Mind gone, they say, like the *Albuquerque Journal*
predicted all those years ago. The judge is dead,
the governor a foolish old man, Nash Garcia's blood
long ago turned to sand and blown away;
all of that I left, and the earth has turned a lot since
(ate its past like some fish and tomcats eat their young
until now it turns up again, fecund as replowed earth,
the familiar is retold, becomes what is strange.
I shiver in the recognition of that place
that is finally myself. What is familiar
is their own way of thinking—the papers,
the trial, the stories told and written down—
and no drinking on the reservation, no

92

Indian can buy booze; the corruption
of office, the two men who left no trace
after their few days in journalistic history.
(The bootleggers, unnamed and uncaught,
untried and unimprisoned, were to blame,
so the papers conclude.) No
redemption this time; the sacrifice goes on.
The night sits soft on my shoulders. Weight
seems gone. Where I can pause (hover) on the edge
of midnight (so that time no longer counts) and words
like *balance, together, reverence,* and *being*
are understood. Assumptions implied
our hands almost touching, draw away.
The self-consciousness of time and place
describing in withdrawal that private ache
moving outward on the dark, to stop, to hold—
arc through the air like cathedrals, left to mark the paths
of grace (the repetition) to make dreams into spoken,
into precipitation, not the other way around (crystallized).

As we talk, I come silent all the way around again to home.
All the mixing (the rainbow ones)
all the confusion (noise of transience)
all the colors (that certain kind of space)
on the way after it all.
boundless in the pausing
motion   rest   accumulation   concretion:
thoughts leap out toward the unseen range
east
north
south
your finger points at the unseen coming light
(the pass) showing sun on saddleback
before its rise.
there is change
and the will to change
there is softness about the stars
like a smile about the lips or
fingertips, like fresh wind blowing
in anticipation of dawn.
there is water, fresh and recognized on the tongue.
there is time.
and motion.
there is space.
the pause.

Surfacing in Private Space

Turning, turning, turning, turn.
Barricades and veils for shrouds,
pay your way covering midnight brawls,
knifings in the silent streets before the bars
close down. I think of haze grown, wine dark
afternoons pasted up on fragmented space,
unmediated. Sentimentality is unwanted
where all is want, driven from without,
go within. (Transposition.) Struggle for technique,
for foothold, for relief
from strange corners hauntingly familiar
in their estrangement.
Time on terms: old ways buy
new times, hard times, news.
(Did I find a rift in the veil of time
arrange things so it wouldn't be seen, I
wouldn't be found wandering along premeditated ways?)
Image of self glazed mindless by touch,
eyes glide by like wet surfaces and grow opaque,
meaning hardly captured before it fades.

I dream of ghosts passed over by the sun,
of musty pubs where huge men speak of days,
where women sit futile, trying to be both woman
and comrade at the same time,
where machines rattle lights and senseless
noises at the dark. Beer and whisky smell
hides my breath, darkness shields my eyes.
I redesign the lines in this underplace
so it will take on a new measure, go riverward,
cowering.

For Friday

Battered and bruised
swollen like an arroyo in flash flood
cloudburst above on the mountain's high peak
rushing toward unseen endings
soaked into earth somewhere downstream
the water that did no good for anyone:
an image. Perhaps nothing more.
Or like the conventioneering doctor
slashed in shadow by a silent knife
whose savior was occupied with protecting
helpless beauty—shielding her from blood
with his body, from sight within his arms
while she held the key to safety in her hands,
secure in her certainty.

Idly I listen to the tales of blood and fear
told around safe kitchen table in the light.
I stand half in shadow, listening to my niece's words.
I do not comprehend their relation to myself
as I feel my body sag toward earth
three stories below. In that exhaustion
toward which no light can reach, I
do not notice the darkness closing in on me.
Later I weep, longing for lost brightness,
dream of golden hair—a talisman I keep
beside me in the dark, unrecognized,
transformed in dream into half bed, half sofa
in the welter of dark furniture I've arranged,
shoved aside.

That dream informs my anguish—
and yours. And the torrent, the bruised and swollen body,
is my own.

2.

An image is always provided, like a dream:
in that dream, the one last night before I went to sleep,
eagle feathers on the shelf alongside pots of memories.

95

Below them you, lying angled on the floor,
your face hidden behind the jutted wall, and
eyes everywhere.

This is the watchbird watching you.

Earlier I had said I don't want troubles anymore.
I've had troubles all my life.
But that evening they returned,
swelling from the corners, from beneath chair and bed,
where they always wait until unwary they arise to cover me.
In that dream I understood a few old things,
pain, and heartache—tracked them to their source.
I saw myself slide once again down repetitious slide
to disappearance.
And that was what you'd said, earlier.
Long time ago I'd had the exact same dream.
Now understood.

What ailment is this?
Plenty in another's life
makes me shrink within my isolate self
believe the foolish lies of my futility.
Beside apparent light why
feel alone the darkness, you and I?
I know the surety of certain words,
have staked my life on them.
I know that love, like brightest golden hair,
like shining, bluest eye, cannot be lost,
however pushed aside.
But oh, I long
to hold you in my arms, lie
next to you and safely sleep.

3.

In the end, I suppose,
it's the uncertainties,
the taint of consciousness,
the awareness of blood and shadow
that haunts the footsteps of our days.
Danger from without requires silence,
a certain restraint that blurs the light,
obscuring vision like mist of murky swamp
where in silence one might drown,

leaving no trace. Yet
in defense of light,
such drowning, such silence
is the law.

It is too early. It is too late.
The evening draws upon me. My thoughts
of loss, relation, knowing myself to be
held securely within the cradle of desire
fade—out of habit, I suppose, out of need.

My hands do all the crying. In the dying afternoon
my eyes shun vision. Memories of other times,
of singular uncertainties arise, like clouds
upon the sky, obscure the sinking light.

San Francisco, May 1981

Riding the Thunder

I

Waves rise. The sidewalk talks.
Misunderstood, it recedes—systole,
diastole. History rides my shoulders
like a dying falcon, eyes darting
for the surest kill.
Andrew Jackson died of a disease
that made the flesh fall from his bones
(the Glory of America) they
tied it on with strips of white cloth
making him presentable for Atlantic kings—
his secret lovers. History's darling,
he marched thousands of people hundreds
of miles in celebration of his
triumphant will: did the kings applaud?
President of the people: the ancestral
graves of the Cherokee made fit homes
for kings, the bodies rotting on the trail
made fine food for a falcon.
Five-sided forms weave around me, I
breathe them in and out. They are the flesh
of the people that I shrink from,
wrap my clothing tight around me
pull my thought closer to swaddle my bones,
oh do not break my will.
My steps are tides: one
universe at a time takes its five-sided fall
from my body, where thunder lives, hidden.
If I knew what makes me human
I would run in terror to the pools of time
and ride the tides until within
thunder and my spirit would be one.

II

In legend told by smoky fires
where nostrils filled with heat of bodies
full on grease slick stew (taste
of corn bud lingering on the tongue)

98

they told of those who rode the thunder
long ago and fell beneath the waves
and on their voices rode the visions
of darkness and no time
the chill center of the lightless wave
the spilled flesh so carefully peeled
from bones possessed, arisen, gone
beyond the tales and time: in legend
the dead bring healing to rotted flesh
see how my hand lies heavy on the air
where living breath moves unseen clouds
where heaving history falls far behind
where those who met the thunder and the tide
forever ride.

III

Climb the spruce tree and dance on the tip
climb into the mountain when it opens for you
follow the winding corridors of winter tales
enter into the moving paths of shape and time
on an eight-legged horse of blue flame arise:
they will not send you back.
Know the silence of dust, the ache of alone.
The sun will stop just two feet from your door.
The center of time will not turn in the space
of now—noon, history, night are
stars, are fixed and counted nails
on the doors of hope, the dying bloody dream.

Sacramento, 1969

Song at Midnight from the Spirit
Who Rides the Stars Like Horses

Heaven and earth are mine
and all the seasons and all of time
and space, and all its bodies' pain.
Opulence is mine, and all charades;
jewels such as you have not beheld
flow from my palms; guilelessness and guile,
strength and weakness, time and infinity,
I have claimed for my companions.
Creation rides my shoulder like mourning doves,
the words of the dying are reborn each day,
and praise for all that enters knowing
fills my poems.

Come home again, then, and again: hold
to your laughter as the dying cling to dawn—
that ever-present lover in untiring arms.
So young then you can be, with midnight's
far-flung stars you might ride eternity and merge
your being with all that you have loved
in that embrace.
I ride forever as a cloud of night, and yet,
like all of light and morning is my touch
upon your face. Here I am
free.
And here I am like you, safe utterly
in this finality. Secure in each word
that passes through my mind, I ride infinity
as swift soaring clouds ride rain.

I am your guide, my guidance you have sought,
and I have entered with each thought the lost worlds
of your making—the sweet, unbroken measure
of my days I share at your request. I steer
the ships of darkness as I guide
the ships of light along the channeled galaxies,
the compassed waves of sight. At my command
the spinning whorls of being you call stars
become the winds I master with my thought,
the lives I enter with my touch.
I strum my ships, I shout my notes, we go:

and all of beauty, all of grace and majesty
unfolds with every breath I breathe:
I live to vision, to make whole
the webbed and splintered fragments of your dreams.
Exuberant and wild with joy, I shape your hues,
bring undying streams of glory to your breath.
My poems are full, my bodies fine and true.
Now let your longing bring you here
to ride with me the flowing fields of night
to hear strong tales filled with wonder and with woe,
and break your heart on fancies of mortality
that fill your voids. You will break free again,
you will again be free, heart mended
with each midnight phrase; each dream at morning
borne on wonder's breeze, you will sing beside me
of what it is to ride the surging waves of birth.
Knowing now where you have been
and where you finally belong,
take up the pain of your mortality:
make your songs of beauty and of grief
on earth. They shall be matched with mine
in the midnight gleam of eternity.

Albuquerque, 1977

¿Quién es que anda?

amazing he was strung like putty o plastique
shaped within labyrinthine memory—
a membering of mustard, seed
of dream, sabio, se discordio
blossoming, este tiempo
pero no más

even so it was just a tiny shatter, sharpedged eye,
skin blue in tone and framed too bright in ash.
no such thing can happen, pleads
no play hay all decked out
full, empty, half quién sabe?
but he knew ripeness—
that, and stars.

ii

in la noche el viejo tattering along oblivion
of rocks and thorns, that harsh, that dry.
landed in a shale-giving blasted well,
stumbled in cualquier pothole, fell.
cantina's jangling jukebox loud
in june, when trees take
misery in stride,
granted.

eso hombre knew it all, and no one ever said
a damp or dusky word. who wormed
tunnels all dentro el arroyo large,
the one from where they walk,
muriendos, made tinder
kind of trap. mi corazón,
este tiempo—idios!
¿cuando ha toda
la gente
gone?

i remember todo a todo; that he almost died there
in the heat of tanto degrees beneath
the earth caved in, and should have.
no one knew a thing: where was
the one who eyefully pinned
mariposas to velvet cloth
and cloying probed
open every wound,
cada lesión?

long the goat man pricks his way, cabrón,
along the eastern worldling rim, aquí.
so very very long it takes el sol
to gutter into dust and glaze—
mira: hawks reach current,
mount hollow deep in sky,
the one unseen:
más oscuro.

was it Old Even So? we named him
from nasality and grabby hands.
one did not know how, when
jabbed—nor see the broken
bitter line arc
to smile.

blue and queer he was and so were we,
and cualquier motion flung him out,
closed off before splintered, spun.
whatever warning whispered,
pealed or pinned aloft,
we didn't know
that time.

Santa Monica, CA, April 28, 1992

What is Beyond Me

—for Marcia

i

"you don't feel the pain
until it's over."
if you
are nowhere
I can put you
where I want you
to be
gracefully
or otherwise
though
I can't do that
which means I
do not make
you
any
how.

ii

I wonder where
you are when
you go. the
sun shines and clouds
come over, each
piece of furniture
remains and you
sit in the same chair
as ever, the lamp
lights your hands,
your hair, or so
it seems.
every morning the air
is as I remember it being
the day before—
where
are you then? where
are you now?

iii

         if you are
nowhere then that
is where you must be.
I can accede to that, put
you in a time and place
of my own making—
an electromagnetic tape,
cellular
too quick for hand or eye
nonetheless inscribed.

         but I
wasn't raised to believe,
my eyes insist on seeing,
my heart on knowing
that you are with me
in the same room. I
cling to molecules formed
in my eyes and preconceptions—
a cradle erected carefully
in my childpast. Girl,
I know (because I saw
a picture of it, an electronic
photograph) what is so.
but believing's another thing entirely
when you're not here.

so I conceive
compulsion
to drive beyond the clinging
specks of words
their obtuse quality.
I need to disqualify
all that we've said,
to investigate what
ever is between us
like pieces of ripe fruit—
delusions—
sweet and juicy though they seem,
hanging from slender, poetic bough,
heavy and sweet with leaves.

I am driven to declare
the silence
that hovers between each phrase
so I can rest,
able to hear
beyond what you say,
what I don't.
need:
a honeyed pear
whose absence describes it perfectly.

Morning Coffee at Peet's

It's amazing just how much you take
considering how many times she raped you.
Consider the antique display case before you
piled high with muffins, biscotti, scones,
molasses crinkles, sugared buns,
the taste of sunlight heavy on the air,
the butter-colored mugs on display for all to see.
Indeed. It's amazing.

It's amazing that she filled you up,
gave you sugar donuts fresh from the frying pan
how long after she'd poked and pried
the flesh between your thighs, her eyes
screwed tight into hard raisin clots, commanding
"Be still!" the dear china, the serene mahogany chest
standing solemn and brooding, immobile—
So amazing.

All these years. All the sidelong glances at memory.
All the uncalled rage, the pain and bitterness scratching
dry sticks of thought, idea, image, abstraction
abraiding; an entire life slowly drained away in one instant's
forgetting, one amazing whispered terse
threat: "Don't say anything." Period.

And I'm amazed. Sent shuttering through labyrinthine deeps
unable to find a way to see, to be, to leave.
I stay, amazingly, taking all I can from her grave:
china, silver, longings toward elegance not ever mine,
antique wood gleaming in soft light, bits of lace,
featherbed, satin comforter, thick coffee and butter
drenched rolls taken in light so pure
you can really see.

Resurrection

he said it over and over I
remember three ways: light
wings beating, gold-
dulled
      sky dawn: old
man, old wife reaching
out to die. Children scattered,
unknowing. And a church. A
dark
blue painting of the sky.

I remember reaching
up to see how it felt to be let
out, and that sky: its reaching,
like teeth that shoot sharp spurts of cold juice
over tongue. Outside
I remember
I found my car stolen on the first of March,
while I was at Mass.

he said it over and
over I remember three signs:
the church had five or six sides
and was surrounded by flights of stairs;
space, lots of space in everything;
we consumed their wedding supper, a
sacrament: consecrated cabbage in fine red sauce, and
eating, everyone disappeared, vanished, just
like the notes I took on the whole scene
vanished from the page.

The death itself was connected to the letter
which could be read as if it had happened later
instead of, as is usual, before it was written.
The bride was dressed in black, a widow, as if she knew
all along how things would be. The guests danced
quietly, sure of themselves,
in solemn pairs,
while the black-robed priests swayed,
facing us, as the rail. Everyone
wore black. The bride more

a flashback than, as is traditional,
a promise for tomorrow. She,
you could tell,
belonged to yesterday.

I think we should have eaten fish
or bread
not cabbage in tomato sauce; it would
have been more seemly if she had worn something
light, or
bright. I think the couple and the guests
should have stayed around for the entire
ceremony, instead of vanishing with one bite
of the marriage plate.
It was when I came out of the church,
after everyone, even the priests,
had gone that I found my car gone:
somebody said it had been stolen.

He married the widow and gave her children.
They didn't know he was still living. She
had banished him to the back of the house,
to be separate, so no one could see
who she really was, or him, and
so he got old. When I found him
he was nearly dead. He showed me his secret
rooms: Doric columns framing the back
of the old screened-in house. His apartment
grown beyond the simple village road she
lived in, secretly. No one,
not even her, could see inside.
He grew old there, beautifully.

The last thing he said was inscribed in a painting
I received mysteriously later on: simple
in scope, the foreground was painted deep blue
and was entirely empty. But it was a code.
He was embodied in it, in
corporated, his words
said around a mouthful of grapes he ate from a gold bowl
in front of him. Looked at one way, the painting
was ordinary with too much foreground. Another way,
he was there, eating, talking, gleaming.
Anyway, he told me over and over: in
the picture, in his apartment, in some notes,

the ones that were only blank pages
when I looked at them later on.
Tell my children where I've gone.
Find the key I left them, it's
buried in the yard by the trailing vines,
give it to them, he said.

Dialog

what do I get said the zaftig belle
of the soda shop town

what did I have said the spray-net hair
of the suburb set

what's in it for me whined the proper groomed suit
of Madison Avenue and 42nd Street

where do you get off? said the busdriver god
with a belch of thunder and exhaust of light.

Eugene, 1967

112

Poem for Pat

I wanted you to hear that song, she told me
so I listened and listened
trying to understand why
even admitting it was lovely
heart provoking
I still wondered
it took me clear through winter
and past full-bodied trees
into another snow.
Well I'll be damned, here comes your ghost again

It happened to be on that day
we found each other again, she said,
and we were shivering at what we contemplated
locked together on the sandstone mesas at star rock
we were looking everywhere
Diné country spread at our feet, we could
hear the coydogs howling far off
and watched the *chindis,* dust devils, swirling
on the floor below—
watched for rain.
Our breath comes out white clouds, mingles and hangs in the air

Today the sun flows softly through my window
and I'm listening to the song,
thinking of her again on that mesa,
wondering what magic materialized out of that wind
and if it rained.

Kopis'taya, a Gathering of Spirits

Because we live in the browning season
the heavy air blocking our breath,
and in this time when living
is only survival, we doubt the voices
that come shadowed on the air,
that weave within our brains
certain thoughts, a motion that is soft,
imperceptible, a twilight rain,
soft feather's fall, a small body dropping
into its nest, rustling, murmuring, settling
in for the night.

Because we live in the hardedged season,
where plastic brittle and gleaming shine,
and in this space that is cornered and angled,
we do not notice wet, moist, the significant
drops falling in perfect spheres
that are the certain measures of our minds;
almost invisible, those tears,
soft as dew, fragile, that cling to leaves,
petals, roots, gentle and sure,
every morning.

We are the women of the daylight, of clocks
and steel foundries, of drugstores
and streetlights, of superhighways
that slice our days in two. Wrapped around
in plastic and steel we ride our lives;
behind dark glasses we hide our eyes;
our thoughts, shaded, seem obscure.
Smoke fills our minds, whiskey husks our songs,
polyester cuts our bodies from our breath,
our feet from the welcoming stones of earth.
Our dreams are pale memories of themselves
and nagging doubt is the false measure
of our days.

Even so, the spirit voices are singing,
their thoughts are dancing in the dirty air.
Their feet touch the cement, the asphalt
delighting, still they weave dreams upon our

shadowed skulls, if we could listen.
If we could hear.

Let's go then. Let's find them.
Let's listen for the water, the careful
gleaming drops that glisten on the leaves,
the flowers. Let's ride
the midnight, the early dawn.
Feel the wind striding through our hair.
Let's dance the dance of feathers,
the dance of birds.

Perhaps Somebody Dreams

—for John Coltrane

1.

Here I am at the corner of Lincoln and Rose
trying in the fog to find the ATM
the Chicano dude at the liquor store on Main Street
said was here. On my right—that's south, I believe—
there's places where I can cash a check,
buy something sweet, get some cigarettes. But
there's no bank.
On my left I can't really see, but
being that I'm in the center of three lanes
I can't turn anyway.

Here I am at the corner of Rose and Lincoln
a couple blocks south of Save-On Drugs
and Kinney's Shoes, needing some cash,
a smoke, a cup of coffee, a break
in traffic, some gas. I'm almost out,
and fog's piling in. My car's a Beamer,
going more Indian every day—
styrofoam cups caked with drying coffee cream,
a bedraggled once white bow from a dead potted plant,
assorted laundry, torn jeans, dirty shirts
in the back seat, ashtray full of butts,
listening to the white lady guru Louise Hay,
her theatrical laugh.

Here I am driving near the crossroads of Lincoln and Rose
hearing her say that everything's possible
and believing that if it's true I'll find a bank,
get some cash, get some smokes, get some gas,
and continue along the stretch finding a way
to turn, to move through the traffic,
a place to pee.

2.

Can I go now? In or out, blue frame door.
Can I find out now? Drive
along to somewhere else?

Somebody's not gonna walk
in this door,
somebody else's gonna stay.

All along it's been overcast and cool
except for a small slice of sun late,
or was it early in the day?

Has it been a simple week—a matter of
merely days? Seems like yesterday,
ten or more years ago,

the air gone dry and clean, mountain
serene and etched grandeur stark
sparkling sky. That was north, I believe.

Or was it even more than fifteen years ago?
I lose track of time, sometimes I forget
my name. I remember a night some time ago,

bombs and blitz quiet for a time,
any old way:
a plaintive, sweet guitar.

3.

Maybe gulls like the ones at every sunset,
praying vespers facing west along the beach I pass
looking out to sea.

Maybe shops bright lit at eventide through leaded glass
beckon serene in heavy air,
hunkering close to me
minutely to define salt-gunned streets.

Maybe an accident of place or circumstance,
the hole I burned in bright silk covering—
blue as the dusky sky—glittered like water
on another day.

Maybe if there were still stars like long ago,
whenever it was that night was dear—
and happy accidents and simple belief.

Maybe it wouldn't be desperate.
Maybe it could breathe.

4.

I hope your new life includes a tree
she told me, and I could see
in the filtered light of mind's eye
her gray gaze and full sweet lips,
patio banked rich,
containered flowers delighting in small earth—
I could almost see the tree
that isn't here.

That voice, long time ago returned
out of the blue, no,
the haze. That time
too numb to quite recall,
sitting there before her, trying
to say what it is I need.

A tree, I remember saying then.
I need to sit with trees.

But maybe it isn't so necessary after all.
Another voice comes through on a line,
other than the one connecting she and I,

one as new and frighteningly dear as hers
is old and true. New voice, different line,
same time. Shift, speak, return.

But you went along your way long time ago
I say. Who can remember imagining trees?
Maybe what I really need is me.

5.

Well.
I got my money and my cigarettes.
Drove back long zoned out streets.
Found my way to the place
where happy accidents are said
to occur.

Above my head a sign warns me:
"The management must be held
blameless for bad deals made at this bar."

118

The One Who Skins Cats

She never liked to stay or live where she could not see the mountains, for home she called them. For the unseen spirit dwelt in the hills, and a swift-running creek could preach a better sermon for her than any mortal could have done. Every morning she thanked the spirits for a new day.

She worshipped the white flowers that grew at the snowline on the sides of the tall mountains. She sometimes believed, she said, that they were the spirits of little children who had gone away but who returned every spring to gladden the pathway of those now living.

I was only a boy then but those words sank deep down in my soul. I believed them then, and I believe now that if there is a hereafter, the good Indian's name will be on the right side of the ledger. Sacagawea is gone—but she will never be forgotten.

—Tom Rivington

1.

Sacagawea, Bird Woman

Bird Woman they call me
for I am the wind.
I am legend. I am history.
I come and I go. My tracks
are washed away in certain places.
I am Chief Woman, Porivo. I brought
the Sundance to my Shoshone people—I am
grandmother of the Sun.
I am the one who wanders, the one
who speaks, the one who watches,
the one who does not wait,
the one who teaches, the one who goes
to see, the one who wears a silver
medallion inscribed with the face
of a president. I am the one who
holds my son close within my arms,
the one who marries, the one
who is enslaved, the one who is beaten,
the one who weeps, the one who knows
the way, who beckons, who knows the wilderness.
I am the woman who knows the pass and where
the wild food waits to be drawn from the mother's breast.
I am the one who meets,

the one who runs away.
I am Slave Woman, Lost Woman, Grass Woman, Bird Woman.
I am Wind Water Woman and White Water Woman, and I come
and go as I please. And the club-footed man
who shelters me is Goat Man, is my son,
is the one who buried me
in the white cemetery so you would not forget me.
He took my worth to his grave
for the spirit people to eat.
I am Many Tongue Woman, Sacred Wind Woman,
Bird Woman. I am Mountain Pass
and River Woman. I am free.
I know many places, many things.
I know enough to hear the voice
in the running water of the creek,
in the wind, in the sweet, tiny flowers.

2.

Porivo, Chief Woman

Yeah. Sure. Chief Woman, that's
what I was called. Bird Woman. Snake
Woman. Among other things. I've had
a lot of names in my time. None of em
fit me very well, but none of em was
my true name anyway,
so what's the difference?

Those white women who decided I alone
guided the whiteman's expedition across
the world. What did they know?
Indian maid, they said.
Maid. That's me.

But I did pretty good for a maid.
I went wherever I pleased, and
the whiteman paid the way.
I was worth something then. I still am.
But not what they say.

There's more than one way
to skin a cat. That's what they say
and it makes me laugh. Imagine me,
Bird Woman, skinning a cat.
I did a lot of skinning in my day.

I lived a hundred years or more
but not long enough to see the day
when those suffragettes
made me the most famous squaw in all creation.
Me. Snake Woman. Chief.
You know why they did that?
Because they was tired of being nothing
themselves. They wanted to show how nothing
was really something of worth.
And that was me. Indian squaw,
pointing the way they wanted to go.
Indian maid, showing them how they oughta be.
What Susan B. Anthony had to say
was exactly right: they couldn't have
made it without me.

Even while I was alive, I was worth something.
I carried the proof of it in my wallet
all those years. They saw how I rode the train
all over the West for free. And how I got
food from the white folks along the way.
I had papers that said I was Sacagawea,
and a silver medal the president got made for me.

But that's water under the bridge.
I can't complain,
even now when so many of my own kind
call me names. Say
I betrayed the Indians
into the whiteman's hand.
They have a point,
but only one.
There's more than one way to skin a cat,
is what I always say.

One time I went wandering—
that was years after the first trip west,
long after I'd seen the ocean and the whale.
Do you know my people laughed
when I told em about the whale?
Said I lied a lot.
Said I put on airs.
Well, what else should a bird woman wear?

But that time I went wandering out west.
I left St. Louis because my squawman, Charbonneau,

beat me. Whipped me so I couldn't walk.
It wasn't the first time, but that time I left.
Took me two days to get back on my feet.
Then I walked all the way to Comanche country
in Oklahoma, Indian Territory it was then.
I married a Comanche man, a real husband,
one I loved. I stayed there nearly 27 years.
I would have stayed there till I died,
but he died first.

After that I went away. Left the kids,
all but one girl I took with me, but
she died along the way—not as strong
as she should be, I guess. But
the others, they was Comanche after all,
and I was nothing, nothing at all.
Free as a bird. That's me.

That time I went all the way
to see the Apaches, the Havasupai,
all sorts of Indians. I wanted
to see how they were faring. I like
the Apaches, they were good to me.
But I wouldn't stay long. I had fish to fry.
Big ones. Big as the whales
they said I didn't see.

Oh, I probably betrayed some Indians.
But I took care of my own Shoshones.
That's what a chief woman does, anyway.
And the things my Indian people call me now
they got from the whiteman, or, I should say,
the white women. Because it's them who said
I led the whitemen into the wilderness and back,
and they survived the journey with my care.
It's true they came like barbarian hordes
after that, and that us Indians lost our place.
We was losing it anyway.

I didn't lead the whitemen, you know. I just
went along for the ride. And along the way
I learned what a chief should know,
and because I did, my own Snake people survived.
But that's another story,
one I'll tell some other time.

This one's about my feathered past,
my silver medallion I used to wear to buy my rides
to see where the people lived, waiting for
the end of the world.

And what I learned I used. Used every bit
of the whiteman's pride to make sure
my Shoshone people would survive
in the great survival sweepstakes of the day.
Maybe there was a better way to skin that cat,
but I used the blade that was put in my hand—
or my claw, I should say.

Anyway, what it all comes down to is this:
The story of Sacagawea, Indian maid,
can be told a lot of different ways.
I can be the guide, the chief.
I can be the traitor, the Snake.
I can be the feathers on the wind.
It's not easy skinning cats
when you're a dead woman.
A small brown bird.

Creation Story

Light.
Stage of dawn.
Opening on new worlds
for the Fifth Time.
And not until they came forth
the Fourth Time was it ripe.
That dawn She came,
riding the sun,
humpback flute player heralding Her dawn
the Corn, sweet maiden, riding
the new day
latest in a series
of alternate paths
time of colors
rising.
And the sign of those days would be 4
She decreed, and the people arising
agreed. So we emerged into consciousness.
Born below in the place of nourishment
where those who have gone
wait, work, and come four days at a time
bringing the rain, coming home.
They fall on the gentle earth, sighing,
the Squash, Bean, Corn sing of growing
and of grace. Pollen on the air golden
in that time, glowing, that return.
So on that day was given all this,
called Iyatiku, called Mother,
the clans, the people, the deer:
tracks left here and there
are signs.

Essentially, It's Spring

—for David Halliburton

It is coming spring on the high plateau;
last week's pink and white brilliance blooms
arrested, curled dingy brown in untimely frost,
though the cottonwoods are hopeful, and the elms,
the willows in their fragile, cherished green—a mixed burden,
spring. One hardly knows whether to lament or sing.

In ivied groves of Plato's ancestry
we are not allowed to speak of beauty,
essentiality, ceremony, signs,
but only graphs, charts, numbers, revolution.

The passive dead revised with neither thought nor care,
biblically numbered bones beside lost meanings
deconstruct in just repose—
futile petals shriveled, fallen to the ground.

Plato tricked us—it was Socrates who drank
embittered draught to history, and fell
into abstraction, but not before he noted
splendid rise of ripe young prick
named civilized that graphic hierarchy,
deemed evolution to be Law: so,
you might say, he testified.

What's gone's not ours to study or to keep: no Socrates,
Plato the Greek disfavored literacy of the phonetic kind;
preferring nubile boys, gnosis, metaphysics, mystery—
just ask the Egyptian bones stored in vaults at hallowed universities.

Far west of cities where *yei* and *skinwalkers* yet preside
abundance won't arouse a deadly wind this year.
Absent extravagant rains, piñons, deermice, woodpiles, and Raid™
pose less threat; just ask the unphonetic
Hataali—singers, rude, unlettered, evicted, wise.

Albuquerque, April 1, 1994

American Apocalypse

Well, whaddya know, and there's old Billbelly Blake
sitting inside a horse's mouth, eating an onion-and-pastrami sandwich,
farting on the lilacs he piled up on the beastie's tongue to make
a couch, and spouting piss & vinegar through every follicle of his
steaming skull.
Aha, old master prophet,
voice of the pentecost wind,
old crooked-tongued mouther of forgotten words—
there you are!

How is it to rest in stone and streaming ivory pillars of high-rent nights,
to sleep in teeming torments witheld from the most deeply damned?
In your obscene innocence you've poured every terror of
sympathy and sight
over every helpless piece of paper
to fall within your grasp
and it serves you right.

Eye, eye
night whirling madly by
never twice the same
don't you get dizzy watching it
trying to forge its everlasting shape
from every convulsion of the god-
forsaken clouds
from the stars tossing retching wrenching existence
out of your every glance?
As you lie still
prophesying Jerusalems to come,
forging voiceless visions out of fog?

Isaiah
Ezekiel
Billy Blake
crying and cursing
grinding teeth in anger and dervishes on every tremor of your lips
watch out:
that horse bites.

Hanging Out in America

Blessings
that rain might fall
and that too
nourishing
the singing, so high and sweet, like home
coming, like roads that wind through the trees,
like crumpled bodies fallen into tears that
release. So summer passes.
Leaves beyond the window sigh. Fall.
Turn to brown, now.
The stranger readies himself for another leap,
counting on this and that / puzzle / un
ravelling. Only for him. (Hope)
His lady walks in shadows behind.

In sleep, the weaving goes on, beautyway.
Old runes broken, forgotten by all but the sea
murmuring against certainty: this time—this
empty space, and the stars beyond, so cold (so they believe).
I remember sweet fair Cherie saying
"I don't believe in God."
I, nineteen, openmouthed, heard her say, "I don't
believe in outerspace, either." God and outerspace, inside
and out, erased with such serenity. But, the strangers
went to Mars, just the other day.
They listen at the gates of timespace for an echo of themselves.
(Is it really empty?)
(Can you believe your every sight?)

I think of the large-veined hands of serving,
empty and relaxed against the late-night screen:
¿Quien sabe? Which way did the truth go?
(Follow the money)
(Turn right)
(Who knows?)

So they are drawing lines today.
In New Hampshire: deciding which imperative to obey.
"Hell," somebody says, "they'll get all caught up
in growth and money-glamour, dreams of big times,
develop like all the rest. You can see it

happening now." "No, says another, "I think
it's time to look around,
appreciate
the land.
Leave it alone. Let no one come."
(The new Walden of our dreams?)
I say, the strangers know where they're wandering.
Isolate, magnificent, they know. And does it matter
"que los pobres no tienen dinero en este tiempo" either?

We watch and wait, wondering.
The time for parting will come (Soon?)
(¿Quien sabe?)
We watch. Everywhere. Like Chinese CIA
running laundry junks up the Mississippi,
from the plazas of our past, from the kivas of our dreams: it's
not much longer; we see the alien way empty, their footprints
disappear. Maybe the new worlds they seek are really
empty, this time.

Bendito, bendito, bendito sea dios.
Los angeles cantan,
A laban a dios.

(I wonder if the strangers know we're watching.
All the time. Everywhere.)

The Lilies of the Field are as Children Growing

Consider the lilies of the fires
feed the air entombing the wind
in flame: flagrant bells call morning
to task for appearing just beyond the haze
of early dusk. Delicate blossoms of air
scatter pollen on the spidery arms of a child,
returning him to secret place damp with the
head of flowers spilled, filling dark.

Consider the lilies of reservoirs, spreading
multiplied forms gentle as death. Consider blood
webbed with spring, with ripples of visible sound,
lapping hungrily toward the farthest reaches
of the quiet storm. Listen. You can hear it come
almost. See the bells ready to spring. Almost.
Taste its call to the sleep-woven child from peace.

See the lilies of the mountain pause
bend, blow themselves into fragile eternity. The
ripple of withering petals rings the wind into silence,
into careful consideration of counterpoints.

Spring comes late to harmony.
Spring seems younger, delicate and webbed up here
where the quick, fragile child can walk intently,
listening to the lilies of maturity—
the lilies of the fires, the lilies of mornings, of the dark,
of the reservoirs of blood,
promising.

La Dieh*

We can say that they cannot die,
and sing of the undying ashes of the soul,
and count the leaves of the gourd that yearly
grows along the fence by the river
whose fallen seeds we will string this winter
and wear as witnesses in the spring:

we can count on blades of grass
and remind ourselves of dandelions
that sprinkle gold all over the yard—
the grass in the back lot is tall and brown,
the blackberry thicket is rank with berries
for us to take again this year with cream:

for we know that we have nothing
to fear but death, and we know
that death is impossible, God
being that mountain we cannot fall from,
the sky being always beneath our feet.

But we do not watch the lines of fire
move over our ground, or hear
the singing bits of metal tear
our children's sleep.

July 16, 1968

---

*la dieh means "come here" in Vietnamese

July 23, 1973

So anguish
trots in his steps, waits
(human condition) under dawn breakfast
table—drops tail now and then on the floor.
A dachshund shouldn't try to hump a collie,
or inmost young go dutiful through belief in finer things:
art is a mockup excuse for life and
vice-versa, or so

Big-Gun Baby, who carries an automatic on his hip,
rifle on this back, grenade in his pocket, knife on his belt,
discovered, feeling like faked-out Coronado going forward into night
somebody thought was day, so he believed. The nature of art and time
is turning.
Bet he was surprised.

Another Long Walk

1.

But what is the truth
to be quantified? And why?
Counted or named?
Idea
logue
rhythm
dia
valuing the stones (logue) the night you say
stars are not purple roses no one
sees them that way so there are
limits
like limbs am-
putated still sing a lifesong
a deathsong occurs not randomly
all over
the plains we could
quantify if we knew how / many warriors died
singing their most important
name
count
which no one saw
in the limits
of their times.

2.

Quantify the myths
symbolic utterance of the Grandfather (Lenape)
count / years on the Red Score
which does not
count for history
(qualifiers)
(quality)
What mode allows me to understand
ten or sixty million dead (records fail us)
purple blood in rivers
burned villages seven hundred or a thousand in flames who
knows in the particular time the sequence undefined, time un-

answered, held in by the stockade wall, the Puritan army,
the Narragansett allies: no one to escape fire or sword.
How does documentation change genocide
into grace?

3.

Dramatistic?
Ritual of a blood-crazed sun?
Primitive life relieved of its burdened
existence?
Whether these records impale
the body of America on the sword of time
all of them are dead
and illiterate (non) the
primary rose
purple in no one's sight
points northward in the cold
unheeding.

The Warrior

—for Ira Hayes

Dayward he crouches, something
flickers for a second in his eyes and is still.
He watches mesas march like disciplined gray and blue troops
into the sky. The order of it. How
they go so silently into the unknown, so neatly
in their terraced ordering.
He thinks about gathering wild onions in the western
Magdalena hills every spring
and walking long shimmering hot hiways
in search of another drink.
The long way home.

He hunches, thinking about marches, lost
in thought behind his unreflecting eyes, about
two hundred miles to stockades in the finality of order,
the long, hopeless years of dying until he threw himself
on the ground at the conquerors' feet and begged:
LET US GO HOME
And the long march back into years until the next marches
to the Pacific, to the Philippines
to crest after crest of blood-drenched hills
to the top of one to raise the conquerors' triumph skyward
and the march back home
to dying, shrinking fields and scorching skies and no water
at all; and the march through hero's speeches,
through relocation centers,
through drunk midnight streets,
through broken resolutions,
through rehabilitation centers,
through mindless unreflected stone drunk afternoons:

In the kingdom of the blind
the one-eyed man is marched out every lambing time
and ritually sacrificed so the blind will be able to tell the deaf
what it is to see the daylight sky.

138

¿Que Cante, Quetzal?

—for Roberto Vargas

I heard an expert say that the revolution is over;
but they're napalming Indians in Brazil.
The dead bear witness to the present in Wounded Knee.
In Bolivia, the Peace Corps sterilize Quechua women forcibly.
The experts in revolution make their peace, relating
at this time to the One-World crusade.
In Vietnam, in Cambodia, in Beirut,
the revolution goes on.
In Bolivia, the Indians die by 35 in the mines.
Salvador Allende is dead.
Pablo Neruda is dead.
The revolution is over.
Somewhere.
The turn is up.
The clans are coming in: Bear
Bow, Lizard, Parrot, Oak, Flute, Wolf, Fire
Earth Sky:
The buffalo dance
underground.
The blue star katsina dances in the center of the village.
in the center of the heart of the people,
the heart of heaven, underground.
Hurucan,
Gucumatz,
Quetzal,
Ciacahuatl
sing, underground.
The past will speak to the future
underground. Relate to the silence
underground. Relate to the legends,
underground. Telling
the stars of midnight
where to go.
The melted flesh of Indios
sings the death songs in the revolution of eternity.
These are the furrowed ground.
The field of revolution.
The seed of spring.
Wound

of memory.
Wound
of time.
Wound
of conscience.
With knowledge.
With Bolivia,
land of fabled mines.
With Cambodia,
land of fabled mines.
The blood of the people fertilizes the earth.
The revolution goes on. Denied by experts
in a common cause, it still goes on,
the blood still flows
the flesh still melts
the clans still come in
the light still dances in the Center
in the heart of Kawaikomu
in the universe of tomorrow
in the spirit dancing now beneath the Plains.
Locked in loneliness
the new life begins.
And all the experts in the universe
can't stop its round.

San Francisco, 1973

The Film Library

—for William Carlos Williams

In the titled glazed afternoon, unbending ladies
plait the light, store it in files too
carefully for living things: what
kind of woman does that? The problem of woman
is the problem. How to catch conscience as it slants
across the page, to know what
to think as photograph is metaphor
on a rebellious day. Half-light, hum, mechanical.
Just so, the line determines what's to follow, inexorably,
like Jack the Ripper on a summer day, like modern
Jesuits: demonless in exorcism, like falls in the dead
center of town that has no point. No serpentlike
circularity, this ambling, but recorded thought.
What do you think? Plate and chronos,
sound and soundless voices rise, locked
in silence, fall away. I think
stars on a cold summer night know
how to move and wait: to wonder when
New Jersey will be restored.
Shadows of corpses blot the screen, are
not to be denied. Poet,
poet, poem, you
pollution of air and mind, smoke-screen, no
wonder you haunt the street alone, outcast, exorcised
from the Republic of glass and steam and gleaming
things.

Albuquerque, 1973

141

Locus

Fragments.
Sudden surfaces mix and shatter, out
of touch. I am deranged by seeing, need
what will stay in line—sights, smells, sounds
so strong that mind becomes unreal, body
a shredded surface, plane and line
angled and obscene. There
is a voyage on the streets, burrowed
in parks and brothels,
peering from windows of flats
and loitering in doorways of cheap hotels
(which is not allowed). Where
are you going, city? Resurrection
and Salvation have no place inside you, though
their armies crouch on your corners,
fill your streets,
ring, sing, chant, call.
I know myself in terms of boundaries,
horns, glimpses of good times and helpless
age decaying in windows, at intersections,
through public arch and private lock on door:
institution.

So this is final, this hallucination:
although I am alone, and so, alive,
I play it close to my chest, look down
and out, look inside, in city, in street,
in body, both ways before I cross. Wind
becomes a scurrying guide
to time and place and sense
of self: the image is where
the action is begotten, and undreamed
centuries lurk in every darkened alley,
around every corner,
across every intersection,
behind every pane of glass,
waiting to be born.

Albuquerque, 1973

Lament of My Father, Lakota

O many-petaled light where
stands traitorous the sign of fall,
weave basket symbols on the autumn skull of Old Coyote.
Night no longer stays the hand of cause.
What innocence could now behold our days secure,
or light cold move beyond the budding tears
(woman sign that clings to eyes
no longer comforted by grief)?

Now come to us our broken victories,
hawks mounted on the tortured wings of kill;
old age sits upon the frozen window sills
and fleshless fingers touch
the careful cobwebs of our days
that hold the butterfly called morning—
turned now into the owl song of night.

I have heard it said
that such poor creatures move in every land
and cast their shadow sign on every wintered skull.
Coyote and this night
be still.
I wonder how a man can cling to life.

Albuquerque, 1971

The Text is Flesh

They tell me that in Beirut
men lounge around the tables
over thick syrupy coffee
and recite poetry.

Not the ones they've made themselves,
but everyone's poems.
These are people who know
poems are words in flesh, incarnate.

In safer, more sterile worlds we sit
lounging over thin brown water
that steams, reciting formulas
about poems nobody read before.

Here we are people who are not carnal.
Here we do not hear the song flesh sings
on its way to death. Neither shadow
nor light are kenned.

In Beirut the bombs. Uzi and oud.
Rocket flares, explodes. Flesh splattered on walls.
Blood flows in cobbled alleys with all the filth,
among which in still courtyards oranges bloom.

Idiom is language of the heart.
I and thou and nowhere at all.
Tu es mi corazon, ya habeebi, aine, ya habeebi.
Here over tiny cups a poem perches

on the edge of lips, stutters once;
taking breath feathers lift
winged flesh into sky
trembles into flight.

Conversations with the dead
convert energy to strength
on the res we talk such tales
the ones who can talk, who know how.

A community of spirits,
kopisty'a, some in flesh,
some embodied words. A presence
don't you know. All in mind.

Feathered nests of minds. Such university, these cells,
these breathings, where wings of hair
flutter and fall to the ground. In Beirut
recitation, chanting. Uzi and oud,

carnal rotting, blood washing streets clean.
Life exploding into song,
chanting. Coffeehouses full of poetry,
courtyards full of blooms

flown and scattered, held,
passing back and forth, flower into flesh.
You know, *carnal*. Like that. *Tue es mi carnal,
mi carnales:* Flesh that is known.

In Beirut they chant together
stylized runes, incanted dreams.
Generations, thousands of them
around a table, chanting.

On the res thunderheads, *shiwanna,*
mass round the mesas
chanting. We've watched them become
bolts of flame. Smokes of blast. The noise.

Seen them become rain. Bring at last the corn.
Here in fleshless luxury we imagine
they're in cause-and-effect relation.
On the res and in Beirut we know it's not the same.

What there is is text and earth.
What there is is flesh.
And chanting flesh into death and life.
And somewhere within, exploding, some bone.

Notes:

Oud is an Arabic stringed instrument like a guitar but with more strings and a
somewhat differently shaped body; its sound differs from that of either an
acoustic or an electric guitar (Arabic)

Ya habeebi, aine means "I love you, light of my eye" (Arabic)

Res is modern American Indian slang for the reservation one hails from

Kopisty'a means "community" or "collectivity of spirits" (Laguna Pueblo: Keres)

Carnal means "flesh" and "intimate person" (usually man to man) (Spanish)

Shiwanna means "spirits who come as rain clouds" (Laguna Pueblo: Keres)

Incanted means "having sacred power to create or enspell"; related to *incantation*

Hoop Dancer

It's hard to enter
circling clockwise and counter
clockwise moving no
regard for time, metrics
irrelevant to this dance
where pain is the prime number
and soft stepping feet
praise water from the skies:

I have seen the face of triumph
the winding line stare down all moves
to desecration: guts not cut from arms,
fingers joined to minds,
together Sky and Water
one dancing   one
circle of a thousand turning lines
beyond the march of gears—
out of time,   out of
time, out
of time.

Some Like Indians Endure

i have it in my mind that
dykes are indians

they're a lot like indians
they used to live as tribes
they owned tribal land
it was called the earth

they were massacred
lots of times
they always came back
like the grass
like the clouds
they got massacred again

they thought caringsharing
about the earth and each other
was a good thing
they rode horses
and sang to the moon

but i don't know
about what was so longago
and it's now that dykes
make me think i'm with indians
when i'm with dykes

because they bear
witness bitterly
because they reach
and hold
because they live every day
with despair laughin
in cities and country places
because earth hides them
because they know
the moon

because they gather together
enclosing
and spit in the eye of death

indian is an idea
some people have
of themselves
dyke is an idea some women
have of themselves
the place where we live now
is idea
because whiteman took
all the rest
because daddy
took all the rest
but the idea which
once you have it
you can't be taken
for somebody else
and have nowhere to go
like indians you can be
stubborn

the idea might move you on,
ponydrag behind
taking all your loves and
children maybe downstream
maybe beyond the cliffs
but it hangs in there
an idea
like indians
endures

it might even take your
whole village with it
stone by stone
or leave the stones
and find more
to build another village
someplace else

like indians
dykes have fewer and fewer
someplace elses to go
so it gets important
to know
about ideas and

to remember or uncover
the past
and how the people
traveled
all the while remembering
the idea they had
about who they were
indians, like dykes
do it all the time

dykes know all about dying
and that everything belongs
to the wind
like indians
they do terrible things
to each other
out of sheer cussedness
out of forgetting
out of despair

so dykes
are like indians
because everybody is related
to everybody
in pain
in terror
in guilt
in blood
in shame
in disappearance
that never quite manages
to be disappeared
we never go away
even if we're always
leaving

because the only home
is each other
they've occupied all
the rest
colonized it: an
idea about ourselves is all
we own

149

and dykes remind me of indians
like indians dykes
are supposed to die out
or forget
or drink all the time
or shatter
go away
to nowhere
to remember what will happen
if they don't

they don't anyway—even
though the worst happens
they remember and they
stay
because the moon remembers
because so does the sun
because the stars
remember
and the persistent stubborn grass
of the earth

Los Angeles, 1981

Los Angeles, 1980

The death culture swarms
over the land bringing
honeysuckle eucalyptus palm
ivy brick and unfinished wood
torn from forests to satisfy organic
craving. The death society walks
hypnotized by its silent knowledge
nor does it hear the drum quiet
to the core.
The trees know.
Look.
They are dying.
The small birds who walk heedless
of the people swarming around them
know: they peck at sesame seeds trucked
from factories far away and crumbs
dropped from Rainbow buns. They
do not fly at human approach. They
act as if we are not there.

The dying generation does not know.
Boys offer me papers that shriek
of impending death: *Klan and Nazis Unite!*
the headlines proclaim. I must be aware, be
ware. The rally forming on the steps
beyond the plaza swirls with belief
that protest can change something, a
transformation needed, longed for,
that does not ever seem to come.
"It's getting worse," the young beard
assures me. His hair, teeth, skin
gleam with assured elegance.
"I know," I reply.

The dying generation moves purposefully:
well-dressed in Jantzen and Wrangler
Gucchi and Adidas, clothes, bodies,
smiles gleaming, cool in the practiced
superiority of well-cut, natural fiber
clothes and vitamin-drenched consciousness,

they live their truth. They cannot count
the cost. But their silent hearts beat
slow with knowledge their bodies share
with the birds.

On my way to this New Jerusalem
on a smog-shrouded hill, I passed
fine stores filled with hidden omen,
dedicated to health and cleanliness,
luxury and the One True Path.
I could see they were there to save
my life. One brick-front shop's
bronze-tasteful sign announced:
Weight and Smoking Control Center.
In its smoky glass I saw
my own reflection:
short, fat, a black cigarette
in my hand, my self-cut hair
graying, my worn clothes mocking
the expensive, seductive sign.
I could see how I am
neither healthy nor wealthy.
But I am wise
enough to know
that death comes in pretty packages too,
and all around me
the dying air agreed.

The death people do not know
what they create, or how they hide
from the consequences of their dreams.
Wanting the good they slide
into an unforgiving destiny.
Alfalfa sprout, sesame seed,
no meat, no cigarettes: what will change
the inexorable dying we are facing?
No rally, no headline, no designer jean
can do more than hasten it.

Taku Skanskan

that history is an event
that life is
that I am event
ually going to do something
the metaphor for god.
eventuality.
activity.

what happens *to be*
what happens *to me*
god. history. action
the Lakota word for it is:
whatmovesmoves.
they don't call god "what moves something."
not "prime mover."
"first mover" "who moves everything or nothing."
"action." "lights." "movement."
not "where" or "what" or "how" but
event.   GOD
is what happens, is:
movesmoves.

riding a mare.
eventuality.
out of the corral into morning
taking her saddled and bridled
air thick with breath movesmoves
horsebreath, mybreath, earthbreath
skybreathing air. ing.
breathesbreathes movesmoves
in the cold. winterspringfall.
corral. ing. horse and breath.
air. through the gate moveswe.
lift we the wooden crossbar *niya*
movesmoves unlocks movesbreathes
lifebreath of winter soul
swings wide sweet corral gate
happens to be frozenstiff in place
happens to be cold. so I and mare
wear clothes thatmove in event

of frozen. shaggydressers for the air that
breathes breathes we: flows: movesmoves:
god its cold.
no other place but movemove
horse me gate hinge air bright frost lungs burst
swing gate far morning winter air rides
movesmovingmoves Lakotas say: god.
what we do.

El Cerrito, 1982

Litany

dead night left its prison to burst nearby in twinkling iron bird-
tone—a long familiar dirge of wet woods

in choosing doubt precious in humid grass warming and like perhaps raw
autumn and a raining forest of this evening to become and more to draw
tightly loins like a cape to envelop rain bespangled faces with flowers

opening beside invisible rain in a singing gesture released as a black velvet
masked the slippery ground and under the trap fell time hiding my face

she would have sung wooed imperious order driven down love on a soggy
moss caressed thought with legs of tuneful winding mausoleums but I
stumbling feet in grass to keep movement forward advanced slightly legs
flapping like trousers of a gaucho or psalm

I arrived at the already diving window to blush and return beyond young
cries to the high area desiring a fantasy legend of subtle ballet words are
hollow explanation to be born

the door began in friendship between thought and indulgence between
anxious opinion and doubtful lips to believe directly was among us an
example of retaining cloisters she said it but the street what it would do

must be imagined the image pursuing my mind of slender silk of times
texture retaining salvation in a prophecy of my own amid phrases and dared
my soul

this hour is no one and of me hundreds of times waking the eagle flew
without me memory of time lost fields rise into mountains to capture change
I lost behind rooms of arms toward sun

while she never forgotten crossed the morning of autumn of streets of coffee
taste of cigarettes of jazz of time half remembered before spring making the
water hollow the crevice a wonderful pool split bark and earth sweet black sky

making my thoughts votive offerings to flicker in red light offer of arms legs
eyes model brain offer of strength of wisdom not love breasts soft strange
moving seas chopping streams to my goal

unimagined ill fitting good in the stoop of wings the diminishing patterns
not accident of asphodel the monster dream another door one touched out of
flying light from dry iron of faith to guess where multiple found sun wings
pure to make me dust doubt with faith

the mountain of marble or pine falls streaming in brief space of her after she came world and life ludicrous now in dust of desire hanging within another at the elder time slipped out of spring

a tepid praise to civil death footsteps the street in gray under a hard sun before she came myself stronger in her truth silver adequacy and equal effect

standing before her to say understanding nothing stars contend for nothing within a special light hidden across vision darkness again gleams mercifully much a sudden way her words rendering avenues of stone a scrap of

paper bright timid not given up a touch now sigh of evergreen threads irretrievably snapped my song turning now to cherry trees dead leaves of december night trees grown since to recall

litany of lilac bushes dying in gardens the rose far away sun birds early morning light of childhood gone and sound cradling eyes color green rain smell thunder on the pane place of light now gray

on me I chant this season of memory of street night of stars around them the arms of grace song shouting asking now and then blocking my path to the mirror of apologetic relations in night friendship otherwise thoughtful hours here there are gone

here open your eyes the chant rises incense without you the shore sinking into birth wanting prayer the church behind rubble of hot sun glinting off rocks streaming light across the brotherhood of saints not left in stone

forever I am without end and ever am the word flesh rising to challenge night the chant of memory screaming high glee gone into echoing yesterdays bent into long gray lowtone tomorrow field unending

she came dangling daylight before me twisting shadows to follow my voice tale again bound to question to time before she came restless meaning clear the summons a message she now from picture to walls guessing wonder almost new

leaning brown-crossblind smiles dangling chord-of-other follow the moment of long daylight eyes roofs are deft movement of shadow priestly temples grooved to waning ears in intervals of no-sound

voice pauses bounds again questions silence polluting mind what being encounters words without renewal dispersed over the original view observed in bending object corners of hands heads mingled occasion of air previously as may

be dreamed in wild history a part in doing not happening proper to feel direction half calculated led to the october afternoon reminder not remembrance thoughts are broken gods dark earth-recollected days silver wheel of truth broken songs into gifts of space towers of tangled grace her beauty glow of thorns of forbidden roses faces the skull in dust

higher I sing stones of years drowning drunken hours scorn behold flowers thread of gloom vaulting blind embrace of hollow hardihood of little men sum of all tone a reed blind language this coarse street love-rude rain burying without a sound

strange fancies of glass grinding pity I sing lips lost to whatever language might have brought scatters creeds to aimless feet of blood when spring is for despair I sing

to die contained my manifold good earth good and I not earth all immortal as myself proved and feels old desire her lie her depths earth life of roots lecture impotent psalms against denial enough for importance

ask reversal of a thousand years apply surfaces speed and twist . . . enough but she sits in distant echoes amid silence aware today because to answer yes withheld her years the blindcord communing like this the boy called God to life I marked this pride to respond

this honor can bestow to almighty the earth in heaven memory of this now where she waited lines of bricks her smile stones changing steps to quiet gold all gold somewhere bread and pyramids stand left round sprawling mushroom for the night

the day-dull hours of tinny vacuum a sun slowly among windows was coincidence orangepeels are back of whose ends of worlds forgotten pearls she is a second-time event a shadow from before the approval of night's initial accent an occulting

word-high heard listening woman and fruit pursue eternity the long windows into space are the end of effect she had words worth gold was water silicone that does not confound strength

chapters abstain from attitude rejected wish lays claim to flesh to stress the ordinary conscious blend to where they are the floods for seven gods and intention

furrowed backbones of wind are lines to slice absurdity lines of white an attitude of revived superstition left indifferent to ionized view are windtowers made by men useless unkept watchtowers aid a web of thunder

the way the truth contained among ourselves cloistered in trees beyond the street to modified grace a smile a face spectre of mind raised above sand before the waning sky we meet again the high chill wind the clouds running down backward over the moon electrifying might then where we were young but now the yellow glow of my shrill mind my thirst quenched on stones

music gone out of sight only beyond the calling hear again the music in a falling star and a thousand dawn light stars dying into better light of her among the gold leaves of dying summer light

in weeds that pile stiffly between banks calling me to gaze into green-moss medley I sing beneath the wind a scarlet call pain to slice dread from souls until the mystery of my body courses through my sullen mind and

living green blown through me at the touch of memory of which is dry but the force of the spark driving me into learning in glimpses I see beyond the veil magnificent folds in the robe where she stood in red light falling deep in shadowed time

I call her name heard her in joy for I knew memory reconciled beneath the call shattered above the sea night over the hills high the fog undone the dawn a glimmer before the face of leaves shimmering

the tide a line of foam an oval bank sand warming the new light around amid the beach wading walking along the crust of foam barefoot head folded my shoulders down into breakwater driftwood black and beneath the current the water dark with drift and reflected clouds

silently was drifting singing my girlhood my soul he destiny of subterfuge wreaths of withered vine alone and happy wind shells of gray sunlight

a shadow a grave passion first night slowly unfolding flowers to stream above waking memories of pieta the saint fallen then below grace into destiny unsought my own wisdom a chaos of vision to snare myself in the world after she came

the word now no longer giving me silence but watched carried me beyond her weeping eyes tenderness I remember and the night of falling stars the wind over the hills above rooftop light

again recalled in windswept eyes that spill God the reality of that now no barrier left between me and my soul

the eyes the seaborne strange tongues and valleys of deep confused music recedes recedes

the girl alone the sea like magic beckoning she stocky and strong her thighs pale round breasts soft like the sea alone the seal alone she felt worship turned allowing me her gaze withdrew and waded in the sea alone burst thought through tide-colored signs not wind now but quick return the magic circle she drew the magic of grace before my salvation sure of God ventured clear the fool's dream seeks little to do now that I come to die I pursue units of memory of God of Saint gone down in dust of her of then what is not now

but in the answer of her eyes designs of living I suspect peace she brings what other wind and stars I before her in the calm night sleeping or at the sky dreaming the grass smells the flowers among the trees the

nightmare moon of grizzly bear the pigeons silencing for night robin's egg a willow tree an empty waiting in the night the silly chatter of the tarzan trees

before her there was lots of time to wait until she came and after she came there was night memory of black howling on the hills the mountain disappeared with the hills a honeysuckle breeze the old people talking in the night after she came

the wind recalled her and the cry of gulls the mountains later the hills what was before recalled her and whatever was then when she came recalled

what dreams I had remembered in morning when bells called across the trees for worship long forgot but dreams in the night remembered and prayed crying hating her awoke needing her back

I offer myself see I am my own my fingers liquidating memory to wreaths of grass odor of moss and slime of memory left by her I speak chattering branches in the wind in black rain obscures her walking overhead

and my gesture I see her a smile an eye walking sit in thickness no darkness to believe then she appeared with the grace of her lying naked in a field among a ravine as on a gold throne born into city light above the crowd

incense and candle light the velvet of she lying among weeds hollow stalks lifting to trees shading us there favored her flight and the white stones pressing in ponderous reflection of her eyes

of the tangible I remain plaster cast herself made the beauty which goes to fingers awakening outstretched arms open halo of light among the weeds now falling away to night

who knows what heavy scents the morning gray light waiting to claim thirst for she was gone then and I had my need of starry flesh when she came it didn't matter but a warning after she came wearing me down to self-pity to blurred vision I to die broken like a wing of horror came to me then

myself you shall my soul observe and summer grass my blood and a vine and not death not word but she here now what memory fragrance long lost the word undone before her breath exhaled

159

smoke chased silk of green leaves and the shore night sound words of no sound the gray around me day and night around me the earth around me the sun no longer the eye of death a lilac bush of memory a gate a room on all sides listening

she a beginning but I no more youth and age now no more heaven not any more not she a dream a memory opposite night identity of no avail that is so

the silver wheel black with years always sex always shadow I heard a thousand longings filter through myself I shall possess the earth unlearned I feel spectres of years lean through her eyes but she is real alone in the rush of streets the supple branches of green trees the good possessed then when she came

Sacramento, 1969

Moonshot: 1969

Had nothing to do on Wednesday
but watch the house grow hot and silent
in the heat. The dust on the TV and under the couch
looks muggy. The cat and I sleep, hot, waiting for dark.

the moon is still more imagination than rock. It is said
that two men have at last soared beyond the heat and noise—
blood no longer heavy
head, hands, heart
light
beyond our sight if not the subtle hearing of the grounded
quick-fingered machines.
    But I love you.
    How equate the moonlight falling
    soft across your shoulders with ash and stone
    so deceptively light, impossibly cohesive?
    Where they are is not where we have been.

When I say moon
I do not mean that dark, pretty hulk
45,000 miles out there, but moon:
heart: a quiet cool house;
children breathing dreams,
whimpering sometimes to their visions.
Moon: a light softly centering inside my eyes:
no one can land there where there is no land
and the air too vague
to provide footing to luminous ghosts.
Moon: spirit of the spirit's strength.
Moon: wandering pale forests,
springing out of indefinable lost impulse,
hunting through networks more complex than all
buzzing, humming technocracies
of Washington, Houston, Flagstaff. . . .

The Source of that light was lost ages ago,
but still spreads toward me, trembling at the
edges of my eyes, always threatening
to break through.   Not
90 million miles
outside

of me, but inside
that light,
frozen on
that moon,
that I do not see so much as remember
as a feeling is remembered: never touched or seen
but heard, in echoing, aching moon dreams.

The idea was not that gazing at the moon
          (now another base, the outer edge of our expansion,
          that moon is cratered and carved
          volcanic rock, meteor pocked
          that circles predictably as our machines circle us)
would drive a woman insane. Gazing at an object,
however distant, cannot drive a woman anywhere,
certainly not over to the far reaches of visioning
where the real is incommunicable and so thought,
by strangers, not to exist. But
gazing into the moon reaches of the mind,
searching with careful fingers of sense-memory,
listening inside the ear for lost songs,
almost forgotten footfalls,
feeling gingerly with the tongue-tip of the heart—
this gazing,   steady, frightened,
is the scape of moon madness, the certain consequence
of remembering what is best forgot.

On television I hear them say
that because man has landed on the moon
he has laid forever its tidal pull on the heart to rest.
Outside my bedroom, late, the moon and I
sleep, and wake,
and sleep again; I
feel her soft light fall on my face,
see the evanescent glow polish your shoulders, back, buttocks,
the lined and wrinkled bottom of your moonward sole
to a dull mysterious lustre:
I wake, sleep, dream.

                                        Sacramento, 1969

162

The Last Fantasy: San Francisco

San Francisco, my favorite city,
where the women are tough and the men are pretty
                                        —bumper sticker

i

In the inevitable city
exactly how we came here or why we
do not know
but suspect each illusion led
inexorably to the next, steps westward
to the northern shore, surrounded by water
the harbor the conquistador said
could house the navies of the world
houses final journeys.
This space strung on
these moments, this now:
centuries of Anglos, moving out.
On the streets people passing—
wannabe Indians with crazy light eyes and ruffled hair,
untamed karmic loafers waiting for the last bad trip—
watching all the changes go on down
playing out imaginings that are landlocked elsewhere
and taken for real.
While here, purified in the ocean air,
shaped by concrete and steel, poured and fixed,
placed into innumerable asphalt blocks, hard illusions
hit by time turn to stone, pave each hill:
we watch the swaying, singing,
knowing the highest suicide rate
happens right here.

ii

In the laundromat two children
chase each other around the machines
(color coded to give the appearance
of cool-new suburbia
where everything will be alright)
and the crazy old woman on the bench beside me
shouts GO HOME as the children chase
eachother shrieking around the machines going around

washing around dryers going around drying GO
HOME
she commands. Her husband, unshaven, dingy,
smiles helplessly at me (hush) his hand
reaches toward her flapping, the children
shriek and chase. Curious at the resemblance
I wonder if she is the Duchess in disguise
and he the exiled Duke, whirled by some magic
to this last facade—but one of them is dead,
I remember, and turn my attention
to the posters on the board that announce
Snoopy Theatre and the Mad Psychic on tape
at the Laughing Man Institute
and government poets who will read on a hill
called Lone Mountain, and as I read
sisters in levis, bewitched princesses in beards,
saunter sexy by, unconcerned that they turn
into this, into that
in front of my astounded eyes:

I would go home, crazy old woman,
if I knew where that might be,
or how.

San Francisco, 1974

Coyote's Daylight Trip

Poled to its environment, shored,
an imagined thing made by hand does not connect—
senses of accuracy in the machine are light
etched on paper,
means:

Bringing Home the Fact.

Men each day go out, return, though mourning the sight:
questions posed in photographs, whether of the mind or not.
And loony poor Flint Boy deranges life: all literature a spindly bough
that cannot hold its truth. Sapling grown in spring is gone in snow,
disactualized.

History Happens.

How it comes chemical, charged, is no matter
of fact but Photograph and
Type. Did they take pictures of Custer's, Hitler's
damaged psyches? I
am inconsequential as the wind. No
picture can be made of formulations called *myself*: mere
corpses show on the plate, true as fact, grow
monstrous in every quiet place, each
institution.

I See Myself as Death.

Vapors play poorly in the light, leave tracings that once swam
onto the page and fixed themselves through careful eye: I
cannot care for this—ancestor's shades fixed on the wall.
I bury my dead. I mourn
for four full days.

Albuquerque, 1973

Six Six Six

dichos

Goodbye, Apple

As I bite into the apple
the sharp juice spurts cold
over my tongue. In
imitation of poets.

The Carpenter

A matter of thought more than fact.
A matter of body more than mind.
I think with my hands.

Bruja

Words come slowly,
one in three weeks:
braiding
brooding
bruja
witch

Body

Geometry is illusion
drawn on a page
up
         side
  down
side   it
dances in the mind.

Metaphor

The form in sequence
is consequence.
An old man dying.
The space he took
open.

At Last

As I didn't know what to say,
I took it quietly.

Albuquerque, 1970

167

Approaches

1.

bones empty on the sand
echoes singing
on the high-blown plains
lonely on the grass
the bent and awkward cedars
on the hills
stark mesas clinging to the sky
water gray this morning
the gulls.

2.

and this is how it will go
wings knifing the edges of memory
blowing clouds into sunrising
like blood on the hills   :
making ripples on the edge of the crest
like something stirring
inside of thought
called *her or him, mother, tree,*
beside, along the way, my death—
or bewildered hands of morning
laid like bone upon the glass.
so blown clouds mutter
against sunrise on some dewspun morning,
or midnight, strewn
with points of reference we call stars:
when did that exact construct arise,
and understanding spill along the edges
of surmise, stalking something
empty and yet known,
feeling like some mythic bird of descent?
so wings beat light into gold
on some special dawning
when not one sound is uttered by any
wind or tree, not one murmur
of petalfall, or single wingtip
brushes twilit sea.

3.

or is it the changes?
not so much lost things
or silences
but what happens when
scattered nightsky is
gathered into focus
so bright they call it day?

4.

they do begin
these journeys
and turn back on themselves
as learning turns a corner
and calls itself *recognition*
or love loops back along
a hairpin curve
and calls its echo
on the starboard cliff
beloved

Fantasia Revolution

We had dreams
about the crystal sun
the juniper wind, apple
blossoms and glowing evenings
comfort and quietude

we had dreams
lollipops and no one crying
no pain—and love if not
everlasting
solid and smiling every day

we had dreams
about great ships sailing
wind filling all speed ahead
never becalmed, no one dead
no rotting bodies on the deck
no witness to inexplicable agony

we had dreams
garlands from gardens
nobody had to tend
ice cream cones piling
sidewalks high
shade for the asking
from every uncomfortable
ray of sun
water enough for everything
lawns and trees
flowers and livestock
children running in sprinklers
water for the taking
every day

we had dreams
soft conversations in
the lamplight, hands to hold
slim and strong whenever
we needed, voices filled
with understanding and strength
for every fear

and every tear dried
by gentle caring touch

we had dreams
that did not include random bullets
sudden death and no clouds
exploding to rain death
on helpless heads

we dreamed we would never be helpless
we had dreams
we bought on time
amortization forever
and no one would ever
have to pay the bills

we had dreams
someone would always save us
mother always did
even when she didn't want to
even when we made her mad
even when we broke her china
and her heart

we had dreams
laughing and crying
talking into loudspeakers
shouting our claims
and never thought how
to make them come true

we had dreams
of glory and taking
down every flag from every
highest hill
and no one would be found
face down in two inches of water
drowned on booze and disaster

we had dreams
that did not include spit
on the sidewalk, in the gutters,
but only clean skies
and apple pie, organically sweet
every day
and endlessly billowing

wheat, and sailing ships
and all the pure water
we could drink for free
and play in

we had dreams
that we could demand pain away
and guilt and the necessary consequences
of our dreams that mothers would pay
if we dreamed hard enough
and played hard enough
and the nasty old piper
never called for his fee

we had dreams
and when they didn't come true
we had curses

we cursed the lollipops
we cursed the ice cream
we cursed the wheat
the cornucopia
the great sailing ships
and the sea
the mother
the sidewalks
the highest hills
and the trickling ditch
we cursed the livestock
and the stereos
the loudspeakers and the glory
and we cursed crying and apple pie
we cursed suffering and anguish
the pipers who demanded to be paid
the ones who paid and complained
about the mess we made
we cursed fine china plates
filled with hard-earned harvests
we cursed love and freedom
we cursed crystal sun
and shade.

Anagram

Every day I get mail
addressed: Paula Brown,
Wnglish.
I read about distinguished lectures
given before auspicious bodies,

or eye the pleas for donations
to United Fund
and notices of fascinating seminars
which propose to parse
the anatomy of God, the Government
and the Student Revolt,

and I understand that the moon which shone so deeply
in my thought has so completely become a wall
just as I dreamed it would, as a child.

(It seems prophetic from this side of the mail-stalls,
where there are no E's on the machine addressing me
but only W's.)

The Orange on Your Head is on Fire

—for Kester Svensen

1.

I wanted to kiss you
        raised my head as though—
my hands lifting
            inadvertently
                    unseen toward your face
and looked away

            perhaps you saw:

I see you laughing
            gesticulating in the sun
wildly in the candlelight
                in red wine
eating ripe berries
            on a hill
walking wind-weary
                at the edge of the summer sea

do you see
        as I see
            you?

2.

a yellow flower
high on a cliff

serene above the ocean
roars as quietly

as a lion springs
into summer

as your face
falls into my mind

3.

We saw lilac trees
        beside the mountain stream
                tumbling down the rock
                    white sweetness of air

          my ear
                    pressed tight against your back
                              I felt you laugh
                                        into the circle of my arms.

4.

It may be that the fire
bird in the zoo
is in you.

It may seem that the green
wind in the tree
is me.

It may turn out that the cloud
ladder on the floor
is a door.

                                             Eugene, 1967

A Satisfaction

The table between us is
outrageous. Plastic walnut.
Christ.
It must be two
feet wide I can't
expand myself across it.
Staring down
you are stirring
your coffee obsessed
with cream. I drink
mine black and scald
my tongue. You shift
quiet as cats walk
on a redwood fence—
you've seen them all, I
guess, all the plastic wal-
nuts, just as I caught
your eyes alive yes
-terday I remember
and rock my stinging tongue.

Eugene, 1967

The Awakening

Tonight
I can't answer.
I'm too tired
to put out garbage.

Or perhaps it isn't that,
but what he saw . . .
and his ostrich head
of hair. It was his hands
that interested me,
bound as they were
with old leather.

Old, old singing
which I had never heard,
which I approached
cautiously.

San Francisco, 1965

The Amorclast

Did you have to do that?
Couldn't you instead
have said Please?
Then I might have understood
your look. But you stood
sullen beneath your acetone hood
black and heavy lidded
as the dark of the moon.

Caught in my throat
your fist expresses the rain-
drops flying around us,
the ivory handle in your glove,
Love.

Hadn't you found
that out of hand
mud and rain make no difference,
or the sky's cold
dull and old
gulled clouds?

You had to keep on
twisting the handle
revealing the obsidian edge
of your intent.

                              Eugene, 1968

You, Like the Taste of Ozone

You, like the taste of ozone
or fire around the eyes,
show me long days in the sun
with sand-pitted beers, but
your eyes don't burn.

The anger in your walk
is black and heavy down the hall
and I am afraid.

But the comfort of the couch I'm sitting on
and the friendly, disinterested voices around me
put you carefully behind my eyes.
I watch the crocus on the table
and wonder what it would be like to make love
in this room that smells of chalk
on a couch as bright as lovers' eyes
as love when love is still possible
not like your face
whose anger has no sign.

Eugene, 1967

The Dying

This morning when I looked out
all the birds were dying.
Several were lying on the pebbles
that formed a small front yard
beyond the plate glass window,
heaps of them, barely breathing
or already dead.
I went outside to get a closer look
and more dropped from the blooming trees
around me, from the sky.
Everywhere I looked
small bodies plummeted, a soft gray rain,
or lay, wings fluttering gently, in the vacant street,
on the empty sidewalk, the aching rocks.
Sad, I went inside
locked the door and pulled the drapes
against the sun that had moments before
seemed so bright and promising.
Slowly I climbed the stairs to my room
lay down and shut my eyes.
The phone didn't ring all day.

Albuquerque, 1979

The Trick is Consciousness

I must have been mistaken.
Taken for a ride, an eternity of them,
masked strangers driving me hundreds of miles in
unidentifiable cars down nameless highways,
dark sideroads of a thousand tales and thoughts—I
must have misunderstood the terms of the agreement
between time and place, identity and surmise, those roads
led somewhere, I thought, and those someones would take me
swiftly there. I must have been wrong.
It has, I suppose, to do with temporality—
sensation, duration, whatever we know of time:
with how waves swell and break, how sand blows from one
county to the next, how light blooms pale and deep
one year from another, yet still remains the light.
I think about long ago
as they say or said *humma ho* when the tale began,
and wonder how the earth has changed, not I but
it in twenty years, wonder at the completeness of it,
getting, forgetting, sudden realization, no
excuses, no surprise,
there it is.

I remember the corral behind the house,
the wooden stairs up to it, chicken house, stall, rabbit pen,
pigeon pen, the high rocks shading.
It was full during the war. My father
didn't want us to want—there were chickens, rabbits, a cow
that gave enough for the whole village, sheep, pigeons,
a huge pig.
They made *chicharrones* when they slaughtered it.
I was maybe four.
Later the corral was empty.
Used to wander around in it, wondering.
I still do, at night, at dream.
And I remember Grandma's mulch bed—
the crazy lily pond she ran us out of,
the tamarisk tree behind the coal shed, deep
shadows there, spider webs, trumpet vine, I
dream about them now, sound, smell, shade and light
so complete—I have changed nothing.

The key is in remembering, in what is chosen for the dream.
In the silence of recovery we hold
the rituals of the dawn,
now as then.

Albuquerque, 1976

Se Por Dios

Se por dios, so there it is. Mama's never coming back. To me.
I've been so good, but I cried, which she despised, she always made
fun of me crying, she'd say, "You can't look at Paula cross-eyed,
or she bursts into tears." (Ninny. Sissy. Ultimate insult: *GIRL*.)
I've kept the faith, baby, written, worked, kept a smile pasted
on my face most of the time, kept on schlepping on
for her, to see my being, actual in eyes
that are forever closed and maybe rotting now.
Four years since she left the dishes in the sink
and went away, se fué. "Se por dios," as she would say,
expression bland and somehow fraught
with meaning—nothing literal—but more
than she would say. A depth suggestive
some call "spiritual," or "idiom,"
"connotation," or even "slang," where everything's implicit, a word she liked.
That, if, but for god, it signifies, the look
on her face the day she stopped by to say she'd left,
se fué, I'm going myself; I've gone myself away, slightly ironic,
amazed "válgame (dios)."
Not in words, but the certain shrug,
the wry almost but not quite grin, something like the kid
on TV when he shrugs at some odd question or comment
made by adults more or less directed at him, "Beats me!"
She'd been gone a few weeks by then, and I still
slept with the lights on, TV going.
A wake that's not quite over.

Sometimes her family called her "sis" and "kid."
Se por dios. What kind of meaning has a life,
significance that finds its way to wherever it is
dead mothers go, dismisses its irreversible act, however
willed, unwilled, intended, planned, deadly happenstance,
with that shrug of volumes I thought was solely hers until I saw
Rosa Lopez on the O. J. Simpson show on CNN—no, it was
Channel 4, LA, 'cause I didn't have cable at the time. Rosa
shrugged, that "humble maid," (some nincompoop,
as Mama would have said, expertise-jockey for heaven's sake),
that my mother'd been a wannabe-Chicana all her life,
and though I was raised in Cubero in the mountains of mi pais,
weaned to Chicana friends, la familia, sangre, La Raza, the race,

somehow I never knew that she was "New Mechicano"
as she would sometimes say, to the core. Nor, I think, would she have ever
said as much, but she was betrayed by gesture, demeanor, multilingual
words, layered puns bounding from one world to another
all estranged, all compelled to coexist—though never peacefully

the peculiar paradox of her position and intent
led her to say the funniest things,
punny in that condensed Scottish, Laguna, half-breed way,
making jokes from arresting confluences
and blank horrors of the barricades
that walled us ever around. No wonder
my favorite early songs were Pistol Packin' Mama and
Don't Fence Me In. I thought I loved their meaning, the joke
and longing each implied, the definition of where
I was, and who we were, their allusions. I see they
were a child's version of its mama's thought,
heart, her nondiscursive life arranged
with elegant finesse to build around her self. She'd quip
"There. That's more betterish," and grin, but not explain that Spanish
says it "mas mejor," and postwar WASP
suburbanites were adding "ish" to words
indiscriminately, like drinks and dinner "sevenish."
She captured gender, class and race in that one phrase
and passed among us her almost cellular comprehension
of the Anglo race, the quirky strangeness that was our fate,
our sense of things, bilingual readings in a loco place.
Ethel was postmodern, forty years before
they mentioned it in post-post-Secondary France
and wish-we-were Harvard, Princeton, Yale.
A half-breed form of wit that shaped a continent and a life,
straight to the half-breed mesas from Caliban who'd lost his mother too
and learned to curse in hated, strangling tongue. Like her
the savage cannibal precursor of a raging race
banished forever to the fringe by old Prosperity, his soul's constriction,
and his angelic host—like her, like me, like nearly
everyone who stays alive, who speaks, who shrugs off significance
along with life, dressed in the fiery brilliance of sunset orange double knit
two piece straight skirt and top just outside the glass storm door
in my empty yard
and won't come in,
who's gone forever, irretrievably.
Nothing can be said does not involve a triple-voiced gloss,
a dis, a subtext doubled and redoubled in vicissitude, circumstance, history,

Four Corners of a mind subject minutely to dry heat and ever, ever wind.
It's a hoot, like owls heard years ago before she died, like, I mean
years, outside the second Cubero house, the one on the hill, the fort, the stone
house impregnable to wind, the one my mother built.

Tonight she interrupts our game of bridge,
cutting in when not expected, commenting, eyebrows raised,
that wry, ironic grin, those startling, amused, cynical, knowing,
luminous, shadowed eyes, her multilayered words.
I said to the women aloud what she said, what memory she'd twanged, like
Froggy's magic twanger back in Buster Brown days
and Let's Pretend—Stella Dallas Cubero afternoons. I talked
about how she called white people "WASPs," spelling out the code
for all she hated, longed for, loathed. And I recalled how much she
was a wannabe-American, red, white, and blue—in truth she
surely was, Laguna, Scottish, blue with cold and grieving to the bone.
"The goldurned WASPs!" she'd say. And, "Blow up the BIA."
Remember when she tried to join the DAR and
was rejected? Even though her great aunt somebody
on the Scots-English Ohio side belonged. Was it a question
of her murky birth, miscegenated blood,
the first true radical I knew teaching me by reputation
and abuse the early lessons of history
of the politics of gender, the vicious absurdities
of the Supremo Race? "There's nothing filthy as White Trash,"
she'd say. "It doesn't cost anything to be clean!
Soap is cheap and water's free."
She was always scrubbing, almost up to the end, if not of her life,
then of her mind. "They say Indians are dirty! And Negroes! Well,
what about *them*, the dregs of humanity!" she'd mutter,
her face ominous as thunder in July.
Oh, she'd curse quietly like Caliban, mopping worn linoleum floor, decked
in pedal pushers, plaid cotton shirt, and highheel wedgies, at the time
some kind of status marker though
I don't know that she recognized her betterish need.
And in the night while Daddy slept five rooms away,
she'd tell in that repetition-mindless sort of way
of drunks and lovers, oh how she had no one, was
entirely alone "except for you kids, and your dad, you're
all I have. He was my knight in shining armor," she'd say.
I was very young with a connecting mind of my own,
so somewhat unawares I associated my dad with the chrome helmeted knight
adorning our old Kelvinator refrigerator. We called it icebox
and like a trusted maid it accompanied her longnight grita

And our squirming pain lit unrelenting
by the single unshaded kitchen bulb naked hanging over us
in summer festooned with poison-coated sticky strips for trapping flies.
The icebox made soothing attempts, that steady hum of noninvolvement
machines so graciously are given to. Confidentiality is their vow,
and it's unbreakable, unlike themselves.

Last week when we were reminiscing about poor Mama's sad and sorry life
the white Lebanese/Catholic/Arab and Spanish-American cultured
knight my dad
told me in English—which he'd mostly learned, but late in childhood—
that my ma was the one who ousted that Anglo guy,
by mustering all the Lagunas and Acomas around and getting them
registered to vote for the first time, and this in the early '50s
and she got drivers to get everyone to the polls
to vote for Uncle Johnny, clan uncle, her mother's brother
against the first Anglo pig as twenty years later I would say,
the evil Bud who had a store and station named as though
it was somewhere, as though he owned a town. He was the epitome
of all Ma despised, from his all but omnipotent position as J. P. God
of our precinct or district or however they made up those lines
of jurisprudence—the white man's legal mode of persecution
beneath the guise of peace and order. She beat him good, that tiny
radical Republican, the avatar of freedom. Pop mentioned it
because I had told him about the JP's mother,
how she used to shoot at us when we played
on the mesa behind her house, and how
she'd tried to kill us with her hatchet when we'd gone to play
with her grandkids in the tiny sandstone storeroom in her front yard.
She barred the tiny wooden door from the outside, said she'd chop
the first one to come out, if anyone ever did, or could. Mama
had in childhood been friends with our playmates' mom. I
don't remember her name. Together they had ranged the hills,
as we called the sandstone mesas behind our home, girls
and young women, when, I suppose, they thought the world was young
and their future stretched maybe hazy golden before their mental eyes
all the way beyond red sunsets on the other mesa, the one across the road
where lay golden and bedazzling Southern Califorña.
I wonder how she assessed that maiden wish in the end,
those months alone and old that she spent with dying in her bed,
chest draped obscenely
with strings of necklaces
and like her past,
especially the ones that came to her from Califorña relatives, so long dead.

She died in California, blanketed in her fantasy, another secret self, but not
one that she kept well hid like Chicanisma, the real reason she eloped with
her shining caballero who is my dad, another almost-Chicano,
but not a wannabe,
from a nearby village nestled in the nearby hills, and got herself
disowned by her efforts to make a dream come true sort of secretly.
Maybe it was that secret she thought would be revealed—
so terrified she came unglued so many years ago
on Grandma's slate patio near Grandma's lily pond
laid out between two lawns, and graced by Grandma's latticed wood
gazebo that hung heavy with bridal wreath in bloom, so it was summer,
and I was thirteen and wouldn't stop sneaking out at night
to meet in the hills with shy love a gentle Cubereño boy.
"Bring me a colored man!" she stormed, "an Anglo, Chink, a Jew.
But don't you ever try to marry a Mexican!"
"Jeez," I muttered, crying, sullen, "I'm not gonna marry him!
I'm only thirteen!" And I didn't realize what set her off
until that astounding winter day of 1995, seeing Rosa on TV.
I'd never understood Ma's drunken fury as she spewed forth enraged,
stark against the dying summer sun, the nearing-twilight sky,
forbidding me—what?:
to compete with her? to get what she had wanted, and had got,
so stealthily? Her cunning, so she maybe thought, unnoticed
over all those years, nearly busted by my crush? Her dad took her back
and I suppose
she thought, until he died
and left her only one dollar and an unsaid curse
in his terrible will her secret safe. I doubt I'll ever recover from her shame.
"I was always a rebel" when she lay dying
she would say. And in those fogged-in months in a California ranchstyle
house near her longed-for beach she told me
how in Cubero and away at highschool and at the university
the two or three months she was there before she snuck out
to meet my father and elope against her father's expressed will,
she'd slipped out, somewhat disguised, to meet some Mexican boy,
a friend from El Paso, Cubero, Grants, who knows? She had to hide
because Kappa Kappa Gamma girls didn't mix with the dusky race.
She was to marry a WASP with prospects,
or an eligible German-American Jew,
become a wife of means, erase the disgrace of her birth,
her early childhood when she'd spoken mostly Indian
and lived with her grandma who'd taken her along to the
sacred dances, the ones closed to outsiders, they

187

held in the mother village just around the other side of the now-dead
lake. It vanished soon after the war, during the decades-long drought
when Reed Woman had once again gone away.
She still hasn't come back, and though there are a lot of flies,
no one has found her, cajoled and apologized for disrespect
in sincere attempt to bring her back. Not too long after the war
Ma's grandma followed Reed Woman. About the time the lake
went away. None have returned, and no one's seen them since.

Se por dios, it's too late now to realized, to understand, to clarify
what had forever tortured her and me, obscure. An Indian half-breed
Presbyterian mountain girl, "Your mama was quite a gal," my father grins,
reminiscing now she's long gone round the bend with her thought
to where her heart had ever been for years before, but who's counting?
Who even knew the secret heart of the woman who made the beds,
made the meals, made the babies, made the home, made the clothes,
the drapes, the cushions, the cross-stitched spreads,
who made the grief, the anguish,
the terrible tearing of heart from hands, song from life, mi mama,
pobrecita, poor little thing, which for some reason I always say
whenever I think of her, alive or dead, something she often said,
referring to this woman or that, like, "Catalina, poor thing." Or,
"Erlinda, poor thing." "Mulbina."

Daughter of the lake, Kawaiku, Laguna,
did you know the Lagunas say "Oh, poor one,"
like that old auntie said to you one day when we of a sudden came upon her
up at Portales by the stream. "Oh, poor one, we never see you anymore."
Crucible of dread and unspeakable, unspoken rage, mountain woman
forever locked outside her chosen race. I can hear you say
as you spank your palms against each other to make it plain,
definitive, put a period on with noise, "So that's that."
(I bet you still say, quizzical, almost invisible eyebrows raised
signalling humor with an ambiguous straight-faced grin,
"It makes me no never minds.")

Albuquerque, 1995

String Beans Being

There's three kind of beans:
string beans, pinto beans, and human beans.
—John C. Francis

the D's they speculate
with mathematic instrument are 3
  (speculums are 2+1+1) or maybe if you allow time/motion—4)
the 3 are: tall, wide and long.
But quarks like poets make
better clue

up
down
charmed
strange
Beauty
Truth

make 6, make navigation from wherever
one begins to wherever one is
to go is possible.

"How deep is the ocean?
How high is the sky?"
the horny lost swains of war sang in the '40s.
"How much do I love you, I'll tell you
no lie": another hint.
  (Who's Up? Who's Down?)
"How many roses are sprinkled with dew?"

or John Keats—soul ripe
early in the season—instructs
"beauty's truth, truth's beauty"
beneath the flowering ju-jub tree

so we know:
Heaven's up,
Ocean's down
  [Thalassa, Williams yearns, wondering
   about the fall he's tumbled to in Patterson, New Jersey
   What is not about divorce? What did he love (?)

Strange.
Charmed.

What sources all life
from Blue/green algae to au courant hates earthwoman
sells the capsules that contain, she says, life.
She doesn't know
blue crabs or blue crows
   (plucking joy from addiction
    to the bright & shining)
or blue jokes. Blue air, blue spells, blue hair,
blues in the night—of which she'll
never hear. She thinks life comes guaranteed
pain and anguish free.

Once I saw some blue-skinned fair folk
living the good life in Pacific Palisades.
They were dressed in green, skin of blue, eyes
composed of Cerenkov's fire.

Down is love, up is hydrogen light.
What makes it all move into the red
and out of sight. What determines
when they join. And how.
It's green, the south.
And up is north, the white.
It's all in the I Ching,
how to cast the sea-change
west is black and blue.

How up, how down,
how charmed, how strange,
how truth and how beauty
exchange
along the mega-micro interchange
and why.

With this knowledge I thee wed,
wu wei, I Ching, quarks & tendriled scattered strings,
cosmic chromosomes, chains of genes
radiative, electronic, imaginative
   (but don't tell)
"we could take to the skies," and soon enough we will
so stand by Houston.

And what about I love you, how
to say goodness me s'truth,
such beauty! Spectacular!

down, down, down
to the salt, salt, sea,

Thalassa, transforming everything
cascades over lip of rock
stony bed that crick
where work and plod
the Sthee, all gentrified—and are they blue?
  (am I?)
Strange in truth, the charm
essential to the trip.

Oh, my lovely, ah
my love, charmed are we and we go through
and ever to beyond such strange,
such light.
I love, the firmament.
I see, the stars.

Up down
Bottom top
Charmed strange
Beauty truth
make 8
2×2; 4×4; woman time all over again
deja vu
the exquisite organized random story
of life and where there is to go.

two more to count: the where we are;
the how.

Albuquerque, 1994

The Sing

even my cells are arcing,
axial tilt repolarizing,
moving toward enjoinment.
the body sing, they call it:
the gold, the bright,
the lesson so evoked, the
harmony. time needed
in integral space to form
new language, the lights
not all on yet, the train
not in the station yet, the
signals not yet go.
but
       hush:
in silence we will breathe,
watch waves roll into shore,
dream beachside, dayside, starside,
count pulsations of each whirl,
that
sing.
indians know the sound of it
coming through conductive ground,
from far away you can hear it pounding—
and as you walk toward centering
the booming fades till
suddenly
as you top a gentle rise, bemused
by star-beamed friendly words—
you come upon the circle,
weaving,
stepping around the drum
encircled by fires of freedom.
you walk to join the dance.
your feet, your body, sings.

San Francisco, 1980

The Blessing

And so we meet again—
small ruffled birds
on the dying branches of the apricot tree
golden in metamorphosis:
honey in the air,
wine in the wind.
Between us, cold and light
agony and surprise—
deep places among the longago hills
things lost in labyrinthine memory,
not quite beyond recall though
perhaps beyond belief. Yet
we return, immortal
in our ancient disposition:
just this way Buffalo returns
to bless ancestral homes,
and long grass springs
again from Mother's breath,
waters again flow bright and clean.
The circles, however large their arcs,
close at last,
reminding us of what we've seen
and why we come round again.
And so memory, that
undying arabesque,
that blue and silver air of being
we helpless ride
forever circles the eternal pueblos
of our lives, restores the ruined
and faded kivas of our dreams.

Albuquerque, 1976

Another Shore

there is another shore
not bordered by any sea
we know
where no fish or beasts
we might name
flit beneath and stalk
the waves there is another shore

there is another shore
one blessed by wordlessness
unfound by any Adam
untenanted by any Lord
there is another shore

there is another shore
of which we cannot speak
though every human
knows its place
that rocky promontory
without a name
there is another shore

once there was a song
faint to be sure but audible
to ears righteously attuned
strung out on voids
and gleaming falls
once there was a song

once there was a song
out beyond blue hills
gone silent into fogs and clouds
disappeared
unsung by human lips
unheard by beastly ears
unnamed
once there was a song

once there was a song
one other than those our parents
and their parents learned

a gleaming thread of melody
you can almost hear
out beyond the breaking surf
the restless arcing waves
sound clearly on another shore
over there, all but gone.

Albuquerque, 1995

Trinity: 50 Years Gone Return

lost finds itself
reflexive
loss redeems
reflex
loss and found
conjunction
the something that exists
noun clause
forbidden
in defiance of nothing
in concert with it
preposition
proposition
perposterous
performed
live on the Great White Way
recollect delayed
signifying
howling emptiness
all bright

but soft:
what opens blue doorway
into dark
leans within
without
reveals
reveille
at the entrance
of the cave
fire light
bright without
the soul
sol
sole
soul
looks
into infinity
eternal apposition
yawn of oxygen, termination

deprivation,
dull rage gone shining,
anomie
left over when
all is loss
still
the need to stay
hung over
emptiness : la
jornada del muerte
the light of annihilation
the time into the sky
a matter of location
dismattering
vastness
cloud comes
dissipates
never ends
earth stays
still

as long as the river
flows the earth
likewise
holy light of earth
cold wind deep below
preposition
apposition

deprivation
empty land to anglo eye
though reservation surrounds
wraps around as hills, peaks
plain, tufts of grass, sand
transforms to glass beneath
vaporized sky
mountain meltdown
cant stay here without protection
prohibit: smoking drink food
within the tall chainlink fence
  of Trinity 50 years gone by
dissembling
disassembling
reassembling

resembling
dynamic whiteout heat
beyond sight, beyond comprehension
watch the fireball
meaning melts into flash of white

just before dawn
two times dawned
the next world
quinto, sexto sol
aborning
om

Albuquerque, July 16, 1995